COLORADO
MOUNTAIN CLUB
COOKBOOK

WILD EATS
CAMPSITE COOKING

NICK COTE

The Colorado Mountain Club Press
Golden, Colorado

WARNING: Although there has been an effort to make the cooking techniques and recipes in this book as accurate as possible, camping, backpacking, and cooking in the outdoors involves some risks, and users of this cookbook assume full responsibility for their own safety.

Wild Eats: Campsite Cooking
© 2021 Nick Cote

PUBLISHED BY
The Colorado Mountain Club Press
710 10th Street, Suite 200, Golden, CO 80401
303-996-2743 | email: cmcpress@cmc.org | website: cmcpress.org

Founded in 1912, The Colorado Mountain Club is the largest outdoor recreation, education, and conservation organization in the Rocky Mountains. Look for our books at your local bookstore or outdoor retailer, or online at cmcpress.org.

CONTACTING THE PUBLISHER
We greatly appreciate when readers alert us to errors or outdated information by emailing cmcpress@cmc.org.

Nick Cote: author and photographer
Vicki Hopewell: design and composition
Casey Blaine: editor
Gretel Hakanson: copy editor
Sarah Gorecki: publisher

Cover photo: Black Bean and Sweet Potato Chili (p. 135) cooks over an open fire in the Lolo National Forest. Photo by Nick Cote

DISTRIBUTED TO THE BOOK TRADE BY
Mountaineers Books
1001 SW Klickitat Way, Suite 201, Seattle, WA 98134
800-553-4453 | mountaineersbooks.org

We gratefully acknowledge the financial support of the people of Colorado through the Scientific and Cultural Facilities District of greater metropolitan Denver for our publishing activities.

ISBN 978-1-937052-73-7
Ebook ISBN 978-1-937052-78-2

Printed in the United States of America

21 22 23 / 10 9 8 7 6 5 4 3 2 1

CONTENTS

Note: 🚶 *= backpacking-friendly recipes*

HOW TO >

INTRODUCTION

A well-stocked freezer and pantry were necessities where I grew up in rural Wyoming, nearly an hour from the nearest grocery store. Delivery and takeout were never options, nor did we rely on frozen, ready-to-eat meals. Rather, my parents were masters of substitution and creatively stretching fresh ingredients. As a kid, I would often hang around the kitchen, where my parents exposed me to a variety of basic techniques, from roasting a chicken to braising a stew or clearing out the crisper to make a stir-fry. When our family went camping, there were no hot dogs on a stick, but rather feasts of buttered corn on the cob, fish wrapped in foil, and buttermilk pancakes, all cooked on an ancient, forest-green two-burner Coleman stove (maybe you know the one).

When I grew older and started going on scouting trips, our troop leaders took things to a new level: Dutch oven cooking. We learned to cook everything from cakes and biscuits to stews and chilis for a crowd, as well as how to care for the cast iron and leave a clean campsite. Eating in camp was not about just surviving; it was about actually enjoying the time spent cooking, gaining confidence, and learning new techniques. And while there's nothing wrong with a good hot dog on a stick, I'm forever grateful to have learned early that campfire cooking can be so much more than that.

For me, cooking is not just a passion—it is a lifelong journey to continue to learn and improve my cooking knowledge and skills, indoors and out. I read food magazines when I can't fall asleep at night and spend most of my days thinking about what I'll make for dinner (when I'm backpacking, this line of thought usually begins right after breakfast). I have acquired a cookbook collection that requires its own bookcase. Cooking has never been a chore (dishes are another story), but rather a way to slow down and relax at the end of the day. Eventually I found an outlet for my cooking (and camping) obsession, contributing recipes to *Backpacker* magazine. There I honed my ability to test recipes outdoors and also learned to appeal to a wider audience, forcing me to try new techniques and recipes that I wouldn't necessarily make on my own.

So, if you're wondering about your own ability to take on some of these recipes or aren't quite sure about your Dutch oven baking skills, keep my story in mind—I have no formal culinary training, just a passion and a strong desire to practice, learn, and discover. If I can do it, you can do it; just be patient, learn from your mistakes, and most importantly, enjoy the journey.

MAKE IT YOUR OWN

For me, cooking is all about learning and experimenting, and my hope is that this book inspires similar feelings in you. Cook confidently, knowing there are rarely any hard-and-fast rules. If there are, I promise to let you know (for example: temper milk before adding it to hot soup—I made the mistake of not doing that so you don't have to). Most of the recipes in this book are designed for three to four people, but all of them can be halved or doubled without any issues, assuming you have the equipment to accommodate a larger group or portion size.

Most importantly, think of the recipes in this book as a starting point. Once you've built up experience and confidence in your outdoor culinary skills, I encourage you to riff on them and make them your own. After all, *you* are the one who knows your taste buds best. Not a fan of spicy? Omit the hot peppers. Like it as hot as possible? Don't toss out those chile seeds, and maybe even add a few extra for good measure. Take charge and go rogue when it feels right. If this book gives you not only a handful of tried-and-true, go-to recipes but also the confidence and inspiration to create some of your own, it will have more than done its job.

Let's get cooking!

FRONTCOUNTRY VERSUS BACKCOUNTRY COOKING

For easy reference, the recipes are sorted into two broad categories: frontcountry (by which I mean car camping, whether at an established campground or dispersed) and backcountry, where you have to pack in all of your food and gear to the campsite. Naturally, some recipes could work for either type of camping, with a few modifications. You could certainly cook up a classic backcountry recipe, one that uses, say, dehydrated ingredients and a small backpacking stove, at a drive-up campsite if you wanted to. However, some of the frontcountry recipes would be tricky to adapt to backpacking, because in those recipes I've made a few assumptions that likely rule them out for the backcountry. These assumptions are that you (a) can bring a cooler to keep meat or dairy cold, (b) have access to a water source or can bring a large water container to put out a campfire, and (c) are able to bring heavier equipment, such as a two-burner stove, a cast-iron skillet, or a Dutch oven. Purists can argue all day about which type of camping is better, but I thoroughly enjoy both, which is why I've included recipes for whichever type of adventure you prefer.

HACKS AND TIME-SAVERS 101

Let's be honest, nearly any meal tastes good after a long day spent adventuring in the outdoors, but a truly *good* meal is on another level. Combined with the satisfaction that you made everything yourself and pulled off a meal without the creature comforts of your kitchen, there's no better way to end the day. That said, I believe it's important to keep outdoor cooking simple, in both the frontcountry and the backcountry, so you can maximize your time spent doing other activities. With that in mind, here are a few ways to help you make the most of your time.

- **Start with ingredients and meals that are familiar to you or that you have already tried at home.** While the recipes in this book are designed to be simple and unfussy, some are more complicated than others. If there's a technique or ingredient that is new to you, such as roasting green chiles or making a roux, try making it at home first so you can get an idea of how it's supposed to turn out before you're deep in the woods. I also encourage you to seek out information from sources other than this book—my way of doing something isn't the only way, and you may discover a different method of doing something that works better for you.
- **Prepare, sort, and organize as much as possible in advance.** Dehydrate ingredients, chop vegetables, remove excess packaging, or portion ingredients and condiments. I like to fill small squeeze bottles with hot sauce, cooking oil, and other condiments. It's also worth seeking out small, lightweight containers for salt, pepper, and other spices. When you have things prepacked and well organized, you'll spend less time looking for what you need when you need it.

- **Mise en place.** If you spend much time cooking at home, you've probably come across this phrase, which is just a fancy French term for setting up your cooking area and preparing your ingredients before you actually fire up your stove. To build on this, also make sure you read the entire recipe before you start cooking; you don't want to have your food cooking and then realize that you need to rehydrate something for 20 minutes in cold water.
- **Incorporate fresh ingredients wherever you can.** Just because you *can* dehydrate something doesn't mean it's always a good idea. Take potatoes, for example; they're already shelf-stable (no need for refrigeration), aren't too heavy, and if you chop them up small enough, they will cook in a short amount of time. To me, it's not worth spending time at home slicing and cooking them, dehydrating them for hours, and then spending nearly as much time rehydrating them as it would take to just cook them fresh on the spot. And when you're eating lots of dried backpacking meals, it's always nice to have something fresh to add to your diet.
- **Taste and season as you go.** Cooking times can vary wildly depending on equipment, weather conditions, ingredients, and other factors, so the best way to know if something is done is to simply try it. Keep salt and pepper within reach as you cook. I almost never call for an exact amount of salt in a recipe since I believe that's a highly personal taste; some people are much more sensitive to salt, and others can't get enough of it. Just remember that you can always add salt, but diluting a dish that's too salty is an entirely different task.

SETTING UP YOUR CAMP KITCHEN

You can create a great camp kitchen and thrive with a fairly short list of well-chosen basics plus a few extras, as desired. Cooking in the outdoors should be kept simple, so think of your tools and equipment as a means to that end. A lot of the items suggested here can live in your home kitchen, pulling double duty by being useful, everyday tools as well as solid additions to your camp kitchen tool kit.

We'll start our list with that long-celebrated staple of camp cooking: cast iron.

Cast Iron

Passions run high when it comes to cast iron, and for good reason—it's extremely versatile, is relatively inexpensive, is nearly indestructible, and will last for generations when well cared for. But it can also be intimidating for novice chefs to start using since there are nearly as many opinions about how to care for and use cast iron as there are pans. There is also a bit of mystery surrounding cast iron, not to mention a few myths that need debunking (hint: washing your cast iron is not a cardinal sin). Let's begin by highlighting some key facts and guidelines to get you cooking confidently with cast iron:

- **Cast iron is not a naturally nonstick surface.** Only the most well-seasoned pans will be entirely nonstick. That said, eggs are the only food that have ever really given me trouble when I'm using a less-than-perfectly seasoned pan. A good tip to help keep food from sticking is to ensure the pan is hot before you add anything to it.
- **"Seasoning" is a layer of oil baked onto the pan, and it is the result of a chemical reaction.** When oil is heated to a high enough temperature, it polymerizes, creating a hard layer that is bonded to the metal. This layer builds up over time (assuming the pan is cleaned properly), becoming more nonstick with each use.
- **Soap is fine, but be gentle.** To avoid having to scrub crusted-on food and wear away the seasoning, clean your pan as soon as possible after you're done cooking. Soaking is not a good option, so if this means you have to do some heavy scraping, be sure to use a wooden or plastic utensil. Never put cast iron in the dishwasher.
- **You can revive rusty cast iron.** When cast iron is not properly seasoned or dried off immediately after cleaning, it's prone to rust, and food is more likely to stick to it. That said, all but the most-neglected pans are salvageable, even those with a considerable amount of rust. The rust can be removed, and the pan can be restored and re-seasoned with a little elbow grease. I'll detail that process in the next section.
- **Cast iron retains heat like a champ, but it does not heat evenly.** When cast iron is hot, it will stay that way better than pretty much any other cooking material. However, it does not heat evenly. To overcome this, use a pan that is matched in size to the heat source, or if you're using a smaller burner, consider moving the pan around as it's heating up.
- **Yes, a little iron can seep into your food.** This is particularly true if you're cooking something acidic, such as a tomato sauce. Some people swear against cooking acidic foods with cast iron, though a well-seasoned pan should be able to hold up to some acidity. You may notice a slight metallic taste after simmering an acidic sauce or stew for a long period of time, but the amount of iron that

ends up in your food is harmless and could even be slightly beneficial. While I wouldn't recommend letting a tomato sauce cook for hours in a cast-iron pan, I've never had a problem with tomato-filled stews or soups left simmering for less than an hour.

- **Cast iron is heavy.** This is not a lightweight backpacking option, but its ruggedness makes it well suited to cooking over an open fire or on a grill, as long as it doesn't have to be schlepped deep into the backcountry. Consider it a "must-have" for car camping.

- **Cast iron is cheap.** You can spend hundreds of dollars on vintage or artisan pieces, but a 10-inch Lodge skillet—a workhorse that will likely outlive its owner and their grandchildren—will only set you back around $20. If you have your heart set on a vintage brand, scour antique stores to get the best deal. Older pans have a smoother finish that is sought after by die-hard cast iron fans.

Seasoning Cast Iron

Most cast-iron pans will come pre-seasoned, but you'll want to season it again before using it. This can be done on a stovetop, but the better method of seasoning is to use the oven. While the process is a smoky one no matter how you do it, using your oven will contain the smoke significantly. Also, an oven provides even heat, which helps season the pan inside and out, keeping the whole piece rust-free. Best part? The process is largely hands-off.

Here are step-by-step instructions on how to initially (and periodically, as needed) season your cast iron:

1. Clean the pan. If it's brand-new, a light rinse with soapy water will do the trick. If it's rusted or has blackened, crusted-on bits of charred food, scrub with steel wool and warm, soapy water. In extreme cases, I've used sandpaper, and some people will even use power tools to completely scour the surface. Once it's clean, dry it thoroughly before proceeding.

2. Preheat the oven to 500°F and put a layer of foil or a baking sheet on the bottom rack (to catch any residual oil that drips off the pan).

3. Rub oil all over the pan, including the outside and handles, with a paper towel. Then wipe off as much oil as you can—you are aiming for the thinnest layer possible. If there is too much oil on the pan, it won't heat properly and will become

sticky, even after a long stint in the oven (if this happens, scrub the sticky oil off and repeat the process). Use an oil with a high smoke point (grapeseed oil is my go-to). This is not a job for that expensive bottle of delicate extra-virgin olive or toasted sesame oil in your pantry.

4. Place the oiled pan on a rack above the baking sheet, upside down, for one hour. It will smoke, but that's what you want—if the oil isn't sufficiently heated, it won't polymerize, and your pan won't truly be seasoned.

5. After one hour, turn off the oven, and leave the pan in until it's cool. After this, the pan will have a good base layer of seasoning, but repeating this process a few times will build up the nonstick surface even more and further protect it from metal utensils and acidic foods. And once you start using it, the seasoning will build up over time on its own.

Cleaning and Storage

Moisture is cast iron's number one enemy. So when you're done cleaning your pan, always dry it immediately, inside and out. For good measure, I like to quickly heat it on a stove or over a fire to completely get rid of any residual moisture. Better yet, rub a thin layer of oil on the surface and heat it up until it starts smoking, rubbing off any extra oil as necessary. Let it cool and then store. Your seasoning layer will build up over time, but if it's been neglected or you notice that food is starting to stick to it, you can always repeat the seasoning process to restore its nonstick capabilities.

Dutch Oven Cooking

Any deep, thick-walled cast-iron (or enamel-coated cast-iron) pot with a lid is considered a Dutch oven, but for the purposes of this book, I'm referring to one type in particular—the kind with a rimmed lid and legs that prop it a few inches off the ground. The purpose of this design, as the name suggests, is to create an oven-like environment, meaning the heat source is coming from above *and* below whatever it is you're cooking. The rimmed lid keeps hot coals in place on top, and the legs allow room for coals underneath as well. This setup is what makes it possible to actually bake in your camp kitchen, which is crucial for most bread recipes and anytime you want the top of something to brown (such as cornbread or cheese-topped enchiladas). It's also a great way to simmer a soup or braise a stew for a crowd. You'll generally be using more coals on top of the lid than underneath—about ⅓ of the coals below and ⅔ above is a good starting point. But if you want to sauté ingredients first, start with all or most of the coals underneath the pot, and when you're ready to roast or bake, move them to the lid.

The process of cooking with a Dutch oven is a bit more involved than simply firing up a gas burner, so don't plan on using one for trips where you're looking for quick, hands-off meals or if there are fire restrictions. But with some patience and openness to experimenting, your Dutch oven will open a whole new world of camp-cooking possibilities.

Getting Started

The first step is figuring out which Dutch oven will best suit your needs. They come in sizes ranging from 2 to 10 quarts. The Dutch oven recipes in this book were tested in a 4-quart oven, which is about 10 inches in diameter and can comfortably feed 4 to 6 people. If you're cooking for a crowd or just for two, the recipes in this book can be scaled up or down and made in a different size oven as needed. Make sure the lid has a tall enough rim to keep coals from falling off, and it also helps to have handles on the sides, since Dutch ovens can be quite heavy.

Next, you'll need a cooking surface that gives you room to arrange hot coals. This could be on the edge of a firepit if you're using coals from a campfire, in a campground grill with the grate propped up out of the way, or on a stand designed for this purpose (see p. 16). Old rimmed baking sheets work well too, but keep in mind that hot coals will ruin a nonstick coating, so don't do this with a baking sheet that you still plan on using for baking at home. Cooking on the ground (other than in a firepit) should be avoided for a few reasons: first, cooking with hot coals that aren't contained increases the chances of sparking a wildfire; second, cold or damp ground will sap heat from the coals, making it more difficult to maintain a steady temperature; and finally, it makes cleanup more difficult and leaves a blackened, sooty mess for the next campers.

You'll also need a way to handle hot coals and to move the hot lid or oven. A pair of thick leather gloves or a lid lifter will protect your hands, and a pair of metal tongs will help you position the coals where you need them (see pp. 14–16).

Cooking with Charcoal

The uniform size and predictable heat of standard charcoal briquettes takes some of the trial and error out of Dutch oven cooking, so this is a good starting point for beginners. To light the briquettes, you'll need a charcoal chimney starter, which is the easiest way to get the coals lit, with no lighter fluid required (see p. 16). Just place some crumpled

newspaper in the bottom and light it. The briquettes are ready to use when they're partially covered in white ash, about 15 to 20 minutes.

Most recipes, especially for baking, call for a cooking temperature of around 350°F. The general rule of thumb to maintain that temperature is to use twice as many briquettes as the size of your oven, with about ⅔ of them arranged on the lid and the rest underneath. So, for a 10-inch oven, you would need 20 briquettes, with 6 or 7 briquettes underneath and the rest on top. However, this is not an exact science, and many environmental factors can affect the cooking temperature, such as air temperature, humidity, wind, and what you're cooking. I prefer to cook with a bit more heat in order to sauté or brown ingredients, and also because it's easier to just move some coals to the side as needed than it is to have to light more charcoal once you've begun cooking. Given these uncertainties, I haven't recommended specific quantities of briquettes for recipes in this book, but a chimney starter that's about ¾ of the way full of charcoal, with a few extra briquettes for added insurance, should provide you with more than enough coals to sauté, bake, or braise for up to an hour. If your food is cooking too quickly, simply remove a few coals.

Cooking with Campfire Coals

If you're willing to tolerate a bit of trial and error and have some previous Dutch oven cooking experience under your belt, consider skipping the charcoal/chimney-starter process and using campfire coals. This takes some forethought since you'll need to have enough wood (and time) to let the fire burn down into hot coals. When you have enough coals to start cooking, spread some to the edge of the firepit, put the Dutch oven on top of the hot coals, then add more to the lid—the ratio is the same as with charcoal, with roughly ⅓ of the coals beneath and ⅔ on top. You'll want to keep a close eye on your food to make sure it's cooking the way you want it to. It's more difficult to gauge cooking temperature with coals than if you're using charcoal briquettes, so don't be afraid to lift the lid a few times to check on things. As with the charcoal briquettes, it's a good idea to start with more coals than you need. Remember, you can always remove a few, but it's harder to add what you don't have, especially when you are in the middle of cooking a meal.

Dutch Oven Tips and Tricks

- Let the oven and lid preheat for 5 to 7 minutes before adding your ingredients.
- Rotate the lid and the oven over the coals during cooking to ensure your food is cooking evenly.
- To help brown the top of a dish (melting cheese on enchiladas, for example), slightly crack the lid to let steam escape, since moisture will prevent browning. Or put two metal skewers between the lid and the oven to create a small opening.
- Make sure to lift the lid directly up when checking on food in order to avoid dumping ash onto the ground or into your food. The tendency to tilt the lid as you lift it is stronger than you think.
- Position your cooking area away from the wind as much as possible to keep your coals from burning out faster.

Stoves

Camping stoves run the gamut from pocket-sized packability and simplicity to rivaling (or even beating) your kitchen stovetop. They also tend to burn hotter than your kitchen stove; the average home cooktop typically puts out around 7,000 BTUs, while most camp stoves will put out at least 10,000 BTUs. This is to account for wind and other adverse weather, but be mindful that your camp stove will heat up very quickly. Which type of stove you choose will depend on your style of camping. If you plan on only staying in campgrounds and cooking for a crowd, a two- (or three-) burner propane stove can handle all your cooking needs. If you would rather escape the crowds and head deep into the backcountry, a simple compressed fuel stove would better suit you.

Backpacking Stoves

Backpacking-friendly stoves range in size, weight, and output, from those designed to simply boil water quickly to a burner capable of handling a large pot or skillet. A main difference among them involves fuel type—either liquid or compressed. Compressed fuel stoves tend to be lighter and are the most popular with backpackers, but it can be hard to tell how much fuel you have left in a canister, which can leave you in a pinch in the backcountry. So when I use these stoves, I typically bring a backup canister. Liquid fuel stoves are more versatile and have refillable canisters, but these stoves tend to be heavier and more complicated to use. Here are a few of the different stove types you'll encounter:

- **Canister stove.** The lightest and most compact option, this stove folds up to about the size of your fist. It has an adjustable flame and screws directly on top of a compressed fuel canister—a handy option if you're traveling fast and light, but it does not work well if you need to cook for more than a few people, since the arms on compact models usually can't hold a large pot securely.
- **Remote canister stove.** This stove uses the same compressed fuel canister as a standard canister stove but is tethered by a metal hose rather than attaching directly on top of the fuel can. This design allows for a lower center of gravity that can accommodate a larger pot or skillet, giving you more options when it comes to cooking. It is ideal for larger groups and is the type that I use most often.
- **Integrated canister stove.** This stove is designed to boil water quickly. I don't typically rely on it for cooking anything more ambitious than freeze-dried meals. If you are able to pack more than one stove, however, it is very useful for making hot drinks, treating water, or making instant oatmeal while another stove is used for cooking.

HOW TO RECYCLE COMPRESSED FUEL CANISTERS

After a season of camping, you're bound to end up with empty canisters. These are considered household hazardous waste (HHW) by the EPA and cannot simply be tossed in the trash or curbside recycling. Unfortunately, there's no blanket answer on how to deal with them, as private and municipal trash and recycling programs all have different policies regarding HHW. But that doesn't mean they have to pile up in your closet forever. Note that the steps below *do not* apply to the green Coleman propane cylinders—you can empty those by using your stove to burn off the fuel, but you'll need to contact your local trash or recycling authority to figure out what to do next. **Never try to puncture a propane cylinder or try to refill a container that isn't made specifically for that purpose.** For isobutane canisters (compressed fuel), you have more options, depending on where you live. Here's how to prepare empty canisters for disposal and whom to contact:

- Ensure the canister is completely empty. Attach it to your stove, light it, and then let it burn until the flame has completely died out.
- Puncture the canister with a sharp tool; a can opener works well and gives you some leverage, but you can also use a screwdriver or other sharp implement. Don't use a saw—the teeth may cause a spark that could ignite any leftover fuel. **Do this outside, in an open area, and away from any possible ignition sources.**
- Write "EMPTY" on the canister prominently in permanent marker.
- Contact your local trash or recycling authority. The canisters are made of steel, so sometimes scrap collectors will accept them (and you may even make a few bucks).
- For recycling, they're considered "mixed metal," which may be accepted by drop-off centers only, so check before mixing the canister in with your curbside recycling.
- Occasionally, some municipalities allow the public to drop off HHW, free of charge, at a certain location. Check with your local government to find out if they have any upcoming events and what they require for disposing of compressed fuel canisters.

If you have concerns about recycling fuel canisters or don't want to see them end up in a landfill, consider purchasing a stove that uses liquid fuel. Those canisters are reusable since they aren't compressed. See pp. 11–12 for a more detailed description of the different types of stoves.

- **Liquid fuel stove.** This type of stove uses a refillable gas container. It requires some extra work to get started, needs more maintenance, can be heavy, and is more expensive, but it offers some benefits over the stoves listed above. First, the canister is refillable, and some stoves even use gasoline, kerosene, or other types of fuel, making them ideal for international travel. Second, since you can open the fuel canister, you can see exactly how much fuel you have left, unlike with compressed fuel canisters. Finally, they perform better at high altitudes and in freezing conditions than stoves that use compressed gas.

Car-Camping Stoves

When weight is no consideration, a single- or double-burner propane stove is by far the most common type of stove and for a good reason: they're reliable, last forever, and are about as easy to use as your stovetop at home. Before you purchase, here are some features worth considering:

- **Simmer control.** Look for a stove that offers a wide temperature range from low to high. Being able to gently simmer a soup or stew helps keep you from overcooking your food or dealing with a messy boil-over.
- **Adjustable legs.** A stove that allows you to adjust the legs can be a lifesaver if you find yourself cooking on an uneven surface.
- **Power.** Since you're cooking outside, you need a burner powerful enough to handle wind and cold. Around 10,000 BTUs is sufficient.
- **Wind protection.** Seek out a model that has flaps that fold out on the sides.

Essential Tools and Equipment

Leather Grill Gloves

I've had the same leather pair for years that go past my forearms, allowing me to move burning logs in a campfire and handle hot cast-iron pans and Dutch ovens with ease. You can find a good pair of grill gloves at most hardware stores for under $20, well worth the burn protection.

Grill Grate

You can turn your campfire into a grill by propping a grill grate over a bed of hot coals. Simply use the one from your charcoal grill at home, or buy a collapsible one that you

can take backpacking. Some collapsible grates don't have legs, which may not be a deal-breaker for you, but the added convenience is nice to have.

Shovel

Shovels are essential for putting out campfires (churn the embers with plenty of water—dirt alone could allow it to smolder) or arranging hot coals. They're also useful for digging a cat hole for when nature calls. You can use a run-of-the-mill garden trowel for backpacking or purchase one that is designed for this purpose at an outdoor store. Foldable military-style shovels are another great option.

Dutch Oven Table

If you're planning to cook with a Dutch oven and won't have room in a firepit or another durable surface to put hot coals on, pack your own cooking stand. A basic metal stand that is raised a few inches off the ground costs around $30, but you can opt for a table-top-height stand with more room if you're planning on cooking with Dutch ovens often or for a crowd.

Charcoal Chimney Starter

A chimney starter is faster, easier, and safer to use than lighter fluid for lighting charcoal, and it won't contribute the unwelcome taste of lighter fluid. This tool is essential if you're planning on using a Dutch oven or grilling. If you're tight on space, find a collapsible one. Otherwise, any one from your local hardware store will work just fine.

Grill Tongs

A good pair of metal tongs are worth their weight in gold. From arranging hot coals to extracting a foil packet from a hot fire, they're an invaluable tool when car camping. Backpackers can find smaller, lighter, and more packable versions, but if weight isn't an issue, go with the heaviest-duty pair you can find, and they may be the last tongs you ever need to buy.

Lid Lifter

A pair of heavy-duty gloves should be up to the job of lifting hot Dutch oven lids, but if you're wary of handling a heavy lid full of hot coals, a lid lifter is definitely a nice-to-have tool that will help you check on your food safely and easily.

Cooler

A decent cooler will keep even the most poorly organized food and drinks sufficiently cold. That being said, there are ways to keep your cooler from becoming a box of water with a lid:

- **Pre-chilling is key.** Pre-chill your cooler by filling it with cold tap water and ice the night before your trip. Pre-chill all cooler food and drinks in the refrigerator until ready to pack.
- **Wrap it up.** Store items in leak-proof containers or resealable plastic bags. This keeps food from getting soggy or, worse, seeping all over the cooler (no one wants a beer that's been marinating in cheese- or salami-flavored water all day).
- **Layer.** Start with a layer of ice or freezer packs on the bottom, then add meat, dairy, and eggs. Add another layer of ice, then more items, followed by another layer of ice, repeating the layering process until the cooler is full.
- **Meat first.** Raw meat goes on the bottom and should be well wrapped and sealed in a plastic bag to prevent potential leaking onto drinks or other food. If you're camping for more than one night, freeze meat in advance and plan on eating it on the second or third night. By the time you need it, it'll be thawed.
- **Pre-chop.** Slice and dice ingredients as much as possible and remove packaging where you can in order to free up space. Recipes in this book advise on which ingredients can be prepped in advance and packaged together.
- **Keep a lid on it.** Avoid opening and closing the cooler as much as possible. If feasible, consider using two coolers—one for drinks (likely to get opened more frequently) and one for food.
- **Ice water is good.** Unless you're restocking somewhere where you can get ice, don't drain off melted ice water from the cooler. Even melted, it will help keep things cool.

Water Storage System

Water is essential, not only for every recipe in this book but also for life. So you'll want to ensure you have a good system to keep your stash from going dry. For the backcountry, spacious, packable bladders/reservoirs help cut down on the number of trips you need to make to your water source and ensure that you have plenty of water in camp for cooking, cleaning, and drinking. For car camping, water jugs are indispensable. Even if

HOW TO **TREAT WATER**

Camping sites often have a water source conveniently located nearby, but to avoid the considerable risk of ingesting parasites such as giardia, you definitely don't want to drink the water straight. There are a variety of methods to ensure your drinking water is clean and free of waterborne bacteria and other problems.

- **Filtration.** Using a pump or filter designed for backpacking is the most common method for treating water. Designs vary from a small pump with a tube that dangles in your water source to a system that's integrated with a water bottle. You can drink the water immediately, and most filters are extremely effective at removing dirt particles as well. Disadvantages are that they're heavier and more expensive than other listed options, and they need to have some parts replaced or maintained periodically. Also, if your water source has considerable amounts of silt, then dirt and debris can clog the filter or make filtering a slow-going task. (If silty water is your only option, consider filtering it through a clean bandana or T-shirt before putting it through your filter.)
- **UV light.** These lightweight devices use light to kill bacteria. However, since you simply swish the device around in your water bottle, it won't remove dirt or other debris, and you also run the risk of the device running out of batteries, so bring extra. Again, if your only water source is silty, consider filtering it through a bandana first.
- **Boiling.** Bringing water to a rolling boil for at least 1 minute (3 minutes if you're above 6,500 feet) will kill harmful microorganisms. This method is reliable but requires more time and a heat source, and you won't have cold drinking water right away.
- **Iodine.** These lightweight tablets take up almost no room and can purify a large amount of water in about 30 minutes. Drawbacks are that they taste awful, don't remove solid particles, can stain clothes, and the Centers for Disease Control and Prevention doesn't recommend this method for pregnant women, for people with thyroid problems, or using them for more than a few weeks at a time. That said, I always keep a few tablets in my first aid kit as a backup in case something happens to my filter or stove.

I'm going on just a quick overnight trip, I'll still bring a full 7-gallon water container for extra insurance that I'll have enough for all my cooking and drinking needs, as well as sufficient water left over to douse a campfire.

Cook Station

If you don't have a picnic table or tailgate to cook on, having a collapsible cook station is a creature comfort worth having for car camping. Even just a basic table will make cooking much easier, but one with multiple shelves or a dish basin goes a long way toward keeping you organized.

Meat Thermometer

The real secret to perfectly cooked meat isn't some fancy trick—it's using a thermometer, inserted into the thickest part of the meat, to tell you exactly when it's done cooking. I prefer digital ones, since they are often more accurate, are easier to read, work faster, and the probe folds into itself, making it more compact and packable. Poultry, pork, and ground beef should be cooked to an internal temperature of 165°F and steak to at least 125°F (but note that the USDA recommends cooking beef steaks to a minimum of 145°F. See p. 155 for more info on steak temperatures).

Pots and Pans

As we discussed earlier, cast iron is king when it comes to car camping, and you'll find it in a range of sizes and types to suit your cooking needs. But for backpacking, you'll want a cook set that doesn't weigh you down. Below are materials to consider, along with some of their characteristics. Regardless of which material you buy, accessories are key—look for sets that include a removable pot handle for easier packing and a lid to help cut down on fuel consumption.

- **Aluminum.** Lightweight, affordable, and a great heat conductor, aluminum is a great choice for most backpackers. However, raw aluminum is reactive to acidic foods and is relatively soft, so it tends to scratch after prolonged use. Look for an anodized cook set, which has been hardened to help solve for those problems.
- **Nonstick.** Perfect for eggs and easy to clean, it's worth having in your kit. However, few options are long-lasting. Never use metal utensils on a nonstick pan, and when the coating wears out or becomes too scratched, it's time to toss the pan.

- **Stainless steel.** Though heavier than aluminum and doesn't heat as evenly, this material is definitely worth considering when durability is a concern.
- **Titanium.** The lightest option, titanium is also incredibly strong and heats up quickly, saving you some fuel. However, it doesn't heat evenly and is expensive.

Measuring Tools

Taking time to pre-measure ingredients at home when possible will save you having to tote along measuring tools to camp. You'll find helpful make-ahead instructions for many of the recipes in this book. When purchasing, look for bowls and cups with measurements marked on them, such as Nalgene water bottles, allowing them to pull double duty for both meals and measuring. Finally, to cut down on the amount of cups and spoons you need, memorize some common conversions:

3 teaspoons = 1 tablespoon	2 cups = 1 pint
4 tablespoons = ¼ cup	4 cups = 1 quart
1 cup = 8 ounces	4 quarts = 1 gallon

Kitchen Scale

Did you know that the weight of a cup of flour can fluctuate as much as 20 percent depending on how it's scooped? Measuring matters, and a kitchen scale is an easy way to ensure accuracy. I use volume measurements in this book for those who don't have a scale, but wherever I feel it's necessary, I've added a weight measurement as well. This is especially useful for when you're using dehydrated ingredients.

Vacuum Sealer

If you plan on dehydrating your own snacks and backpacking meals, the best way to keep them fresh is to use a vacuum sealer. Bacteria need oxygen to survive, and a vacuum sealer deprives them of that better than any zip-top bag or other container can. In addition to keeping your food fresh, it allows you to customize portions and pack them into compact, well-sealed packages, useful for when you've had a long day on the trail and don't feel like spending time carefully measuring ingredients. The empty bags are also handy for packing out trash.

Mandoline Slicer

When dehydrating fruits and vegetables, it's important to ensure you have thin, uniform slices so your batch dehydrates evenly. A mandoline slicer makes quick work of that task, leaving you with a batch of food evenly sliced in no time. It's worth buying one with a hand guard to protect your hands (trust me, you'll end up saving money on bandages and/or stitches—your knuckles will thank you).

Skewers

Whether metal or bamboo, I keep a few skewers stashed with my car-camping gear. They're essential for kebabs, but they also work as a marshmallow-roasting stick in a pinch or for propping open your Dutch oven to let steam escape.

BUILDING YOUR PANTRY

Getting organized for a camping trip, packing up, and deciding what to cook and how to cook it definitely takes some forethought and planning. To help take some of the stress out of that prep, consider keeping your home pantry stocked with some favorite shelf-stable essentials. You'll notice that a few ingredients pop up frequently throughout this book. These are some of the ingredients I rely on to cut down on weight and bulk while still ending up with a flavorful, satisfying meal. You'll find several of those on this list.

Bouillon Cubes

Several recipes in this book call for bouillon cubes, which are dried, concentrated blocks made from chicken, beef, or vegetable stock. Lightweight and compact, they are an easy way to give soup, sauce, or stew an extra savory depth. While the standard is to use one cube to make one cup of broth, that ratio can vary slightly among brands (especially with some vegetarian and vegan brands). Unless otherwise specified, the 1-to-1 ratio is the rule of thumb that I follow in this book. You'll note that recipes don't specify which type of bouillon to use; I've left that up to you. Chicken bouillon goes with just about anything, but there are excellent vegetarian and vegan options (as well as gluten-free options). Whichever type you pick, keep in mind that you may need to use more or less of a certain brand to reconstitute a cup of broth.

Dehydrated/Freeze-Dried Ingredients

When a recipe calls for dehydrated or dried ingredients, you'll find a corresponding recipe for that ingredient in the dehydrator chapter (see p. 35). However, if you are looking to save time or aren't ready to invest in a dehydrator, you should be able to find those ingredients at a grocery store, outdoor store, or online. Mushrooms, for example, are widely available dried (Asian grocery stores often sell dried shiitake and oyster mushrooms in large quantities for a reasonable price). Freeze-dried beans and vegetables can also be substituted for their dehydrated counterparts. You'll also notice that a few recipes call for nori, or dried seaweed. This can be found in many grocery stores and is a great lightweight ingredient for adding savory depth to some dishes.

Canned/Packaged Meats and Seafood

Tuna, salmon, and smoked oysters and mussels all come in handy packets or tins to keep in your pantry. It's always worth throwing a few into your backpack as an emergency stash. Packable, shelf-stable, ready-to-eat, and high in protein, they are light to carry and make a quick lunch or ready-made snack. They are also easy to add to pasta, soups, and rice dishes for an extra punch of protein when you need it.

Milk Powder

When you can't tote a cooler along on your trip or you simply prefer to leave space in there for other food and drinks, dried milk and buttermilk powders are the perfect shelf-stable solutions for bringing dairy. Coconut milk powder can make for a good nondairy substitute, but keep in mind that it will impart some coconut flavor to the dish. As with bouillon cubes, the amount of milk powder used will depend on the specific brand you prefer. If the recipe calls for one cup of liquid milk, follow the reconstitution directions on the package for best results.

Oils

Not all oils are created equal, and some work better for adding flavor than for sautéing. Oils with high smoke points are best for sautéing and frying; when an oil begins to smoke, it becomes bitter and acrid, and any distinct flavor it has will be lost. Here are a few common oils and their uses, from neutral-flavored cooking oils to those better suited to flavoring a dish:

Neutral Oils (best for cooking)

- **Regular olive oil.** More processed than its extra-virgin counterpart, this makes a good all-around cooking oil.
- **Vegetable oil.** This neutral-tasting oil is a good all-purpose cooking oil, with a slightly higher smoke point than regular olive oil.
- **Grapeseed oil.** Neutral-tasting and with a very high smoke point, this is not only a good cooking oil but is also my go-to for seasoning cast iron.
- **Peanut oil.** This is another good option for a neutral-tasting, all-purpose cooking oil with a high smoke point.
- **Canola oil.** Similar to vegetable oil, this neutral-tasting, all-purpose oil has a lower smoke point than grapeseed or peanut oil.
- **Avocado oil.** This oil has the highest smoke point on this list and is neutral-tasting but can be expensive and difficult to find in stores.

Oils with a Stronger Flavor (best for imparting a certain taste or adding near the end of cooking)

- **Coconut oil.** This oil can impart a slight coconut taste to foods, so use it in dishes where it is a complimentary flavor, such as in curry or sweets. At room temperature, it's solid, so it can be difficult to use if you need to mix it into a batter or dough.
- **Sesame oil.** This oil is best used to flavor a dish rather than to sauté or fry ingredients since its delicate, nuanced flavor will be lost when it's heated.
- **Extra-virgin olive oil.** This is the least processed and most unrefined type of olive oil, with a strong, grassy flavor. It's best used to drizzle over pasta or in salad dressings since heat will diminish its flavor, and it has a low smoke point. It also tends to be the priciest oil on this list.

Condiments

Some condiments you just can't live without (for me, that's hot sauce). Here are a few you may want to throw into your pack or cooler:

- **Soy sauce (or tamari, which is gluten-free).** This is a good way to add salt and savory depth to meals. While great in Asian dishes, know that nearly any soup or stew can benefit from a few drops. For easy packing, look for individual packets sold in bulk.

- **Hot sauce.** I won't leave home without it. Sriracha is my go-to for Asian dishes, Tapatío or Cholula for Latin American dishes, and Crystal for a Louisiana-style hot sauce. A small squirt bottle for backpacking keeps the liquid contained and cuts down on weight.
- **Vinegars.** A little vinegar goes a long way and adds a crucial element to many soups, stews, and sauces. I carry a small amount of rice vinegar or apple cider vinegar, which aren't as harsh as white vinegar and have more flavor, in case a dish needs a little extra kick (but use it sparingly).

Spices

Salt and pepper are nonnegotiable, but several other dried herbs and spices will definitely earn their keep on your pantry shelf. Having them on hand (I use small plastic spice containers made for backpacking) gives you room to experiment and adjust recipes to your own tastes. I use the following liberally and often in my own cooking, and they appear frequently in the recipes in this book:

basil	ginger
cayenne	minced onion
coriander	oregano
cumin	paprika
curry powder	red pepper flakes
garlic powder	turmeric

SEVEN PRINCIPLES OF LEAVE NO TRACE

No one likes rolling up to a campsite only to see a pile of other peoples' trash. And as our public lands see increasing use, it's more important than ever to pitch in and do your part to leave the wild a little bit better than the way you found it. The Leave No Trace Center for Outdoor Ethics (lnt.org), which was built on a "no trace" program developed by the US Forest Service in the 1980s, is the guiding light when it comes to how to recreate responsibly. The nonprofit formed in 1994 to carry on research and education in the spirit of the program. The organization has developed seven guiding principles, which can be applied in a variety of different ways when it comes to feeding yourself in the wild.

Plan Ahead and Prepare

Planning ahead is not only the best way to make sure your meals turn out well, it also helps you minimize your impact on the land and wildlife. Here are some tips to help you prepare:

- If you plan on using a campfire to cook your meals, make sure there is already an established fire ring and check for any fire restrictions with the local sheriff's office. During the hot summer months, it's common for there to be a complete ban on open fires, which includes charcoal burning as well. This is the time to dust off your two-burner propane or compressed gas stove.
- If possible, purchase firewood close to your campsite. Transporting firewood long distances can spread tree-killing insects and diseases to new areas. If you're wondering where to find firewood locally, visit dontmovefirewood.org for a list of resources.
- If bear canisters are not required and you don't have access to one, bring enough rope to hang a food bag if you need to keep your food away from critters (see p. 30).
- Bring extra zip-top or other leak-proof bags to pack out your trash (or for extra karma points, to pack out someone else's).
- Remove excess packaging ahead of time and consolidate as many ingredients as possible to cut down on the trash you'll need to pack out.

Travel and Camp on Durable Surfaces

Choosing a backcountry campsite is one of the highest-impact choices you have to make. Choosing wisely will help you minimize any impact from your cooking activity.

- Avoid setting up your camp or cooking area on fragile surfaces, especially in high alpine tundra or on cryptobiotic soil in the desert. Rock, sand, and gravel are the most durable surfaces and can handle repeated trampling.
- If possible, choose a site that is already impacted rather than making a new one, especially if there is already an established fire ring.
- Set up camp at least 200 feet away from a water source in order to allow wildlife access. About 70 steps is a good rule of thumb.

- Concentrate your cooking area and other high-traffic routes to keep your footprint as small as possible. Bring a large water reservoir, such as a lightweight, packable bladder, to cut down on the number of trips you need to make to a water source. By limiting your time at a water source, you reduce the trampling impact and give wildlife more opportunities to access it undisturbed.
- If you're using a Dutch oven, use it in an established firepit or grill, or bring your own surface that is designed for that use.

Dispose of Waste Properly

Doing the dishes is everyone's least-favorite task, but making sure they're done right will lessen your impact on water sources and also keep critters, large and small, away from your camp.

- Pack it in, pack it out.
- Don't wash your dishes directly in natural water sources, such as lakes and rivers.
- Avoid using soap as much as possible—even biodegradable soaps can be harmful to fish and wildlife. Boiling water in the dirty pot is a good way to remove stubborn bits of food.
- Strain bits of food out of your dishwater and dump them into your trash bag. Scatter the dishwater at least 200 feet away from your campsite or any water sources.
- Use hand sanitizer to cut down on soap and wastewater.
- Burning your trash is not a viable way of getting rid of it. Half-burned food scraps and trash are not only unpleasant for the next group of campers but can be harmful to wildlife. And any packaging containing foil won't burn completely.

Leave What You Find

Leave a campsite in as good or better shape than you found it.

- Don't create new fire rings.
- Leave properly-built fire rings in place; dismantling one could cause the next campers to build a new one in a different spot, impacting the site further.
- Leave natural objects where they are, as they could be benefiting other plants or wildlife.

Minimize Campfire Impacts

It may seem unfathomable for most people to camp without a campfire, but you should carefully consider whether you need one or not. Most of the recipes in this book are designed for cooking without an open fire or charcoal. Much of the western US is suffering from severe drought, and an unattended campfire can easily spark a major wildfire. Additionally, overcollection of firewood from mountain environments has a significant ecological impact. If you're planning on using a fire for cooking or warmth, plan ahead to see if there is already an established fire ring at your campsite. Otherwise, consider bringing your own stove.

- Check local fire conditions or restrictions before planning your meals.
- Use established fire rings or bring a fire pan, especially if camping in delicate areas, such as deserts or high alpine tundra.
- Collect dead wood on the ground from a large area away from your campsite; don't pull branches from standing or fallen trees, as these can be providing shelter for wildlife or could be crucial to a standing tree's survival.
- Purchase wood locally, or gather it at your campsite, to avoid transporting tree-killing insects.
- If gathering firewood, use small pieces, about the diameter of your wrist.
- Burn your wood down to white ash, and scatter any unused/unburned pieces in a wide area around your campsite.
- Put your fire out with water, not dirt; a fire can smolder underground for months, even through a winter.
- Make sure your fire is dead out when you leave it; that means it should be cool to the touch.

Respect Wildlife

Remember, when you're out in the wild, you're a guest in their home. Aside from never feeding wildlife, here are a few ways you can help keep them wild.

- Set up your campsite at least 200 feet away from a water source to allow access for animals.
- Keep your campsite clean and pick up any food scraps.

- Pack out all trash and food scraps, including fruit peels and strained bits from your dishwater.
- Fill up your water reservoirs before dark to avoid visiting a water source at night, when many animals are active.
- Properly store your food, with extra precautions in bear habitat.

Be Considerate of Other Visitors

Last but not least—and not limited to your cooking—act in a way that allows others to enjoy the outdoors. By following the previous guidelines, you're ensuring that whoever comes after you will have an enjoyable outdoor experience. By being a good steward of the land, you're also doing your part to keep access to wild places open.

HOW TO STORE FOOD IN BEAR COUNTRY

Bears can sense a smell up to 20 miles away, so when you're camping in bear habitat, it's crucial to keep food properly stored. Many national parks and wilderness areas require the use of bear-resistant canisters, which can often be rented. Store all food, trash, and *anything* with a scent (toothpaste, gum, deodorant, soap, clothing used to cook in, etc.) in a bear-resistant canister (or the metal locker at a developed campground) or in a hard-sided vehicle with the windows completely closed.

If you're using a canister, place it at least 100 yards from your campsite and away from any slopes, cliffs, or running water where a bear could roll it away. If you aren't required to use a canister—check regulations in the area you're camping in—then a bear hang is your next best option for storing food, trash, and scented items. Hang a bag at least 100 yards away from your campsite. It should be at least 10 feet off the ground and 4 feet away from other branches. Be sure to bring an extra stuff sack or dry bag to put your food in as well as sufficient rope and a carabiner to hang the bag (about 50 feet of paracord is sufficient). A nylon stuff sack with a drawstring will work, but if there's a chance for rain, I prefer to use a waterproof dry bag. It's also a good idea to carry bear spray—make sure that it's easily accessible and you know how to use it.

PACKING CHECKLISTS

In my experience, some of the most essential items are the easiest to forget. When you're packing a new lightweight sleeping bag or other fancy new gear, things like toilet paper and trash bags tend to be at the back of your mind. So I rely on a system where I keep some easy-to-forget essentials packed in a stuff sack or plastic tub at all times. I call it my go-box. When I return from a trip, I clean or refresh items as needed, and then repack them so the box is always packed and ready to go the next time I am. Here's what's in my go-box, as well as other essentials to pack:

BACKPACKING

GO-BOX

- salt and pepper
- paracord
- biodegradable soap
- toilet paper
- extra fuel
- headlamp (and extra batteries)
- extra utensils
- lightweight cutting board
- lighter/matches
- trash bags
- newspaper (for starting fires)
- resealable plastic bags

COMPLETE CHECKLIST

- trash bags
- biodegradable soap (such as Campsuds or Wilderness Wash)
- hand sanitizer
- extra stove fuel
- fire starters (matches and/or lighters, and maybe some newspaper)
- basic spices (at the very least, salt and pepper)
- cooking oil
- plates/bowls
- eating utensils
- toilet paper
- paracord (for bear hangs)
- packable stuff sack or dry bag (for bear hangs)
- resealable plastic bags
- multi-tool or knife
- cutting board
- water filter
- packable water reservoir

CAR CAMPING

In addition to what's on the backpacking list, I keep these items in a plastic storage box for car camping:

GO-BOX

- paper towels
- hatchet
- aluminum foil
- metal grill tongs
- leather gloves
- plastic egg carrier
- bamboo or metal skewers

COMPLETE CHECKLIST

- trash bags
- plates/bowls/utensils
- aluminum foil
- paper towels/reusable washcloths
- biodegradable soap (such as Campsuds or Wilderness Wash)
- metal tongs
- extra stove fuel
- grill grate
- grill gloves
- cutting board
- knife
- hatchet
- fire starters (matches and/or lighters, and maybe some newspaper)
- basic spices (at the very least, salt and pepper)
- cooking oil
- paper plates and plastic utensils
- toilet paper
- resealable plastic bags
- hand sanitizer
- rope or paracord
- water container, full of fresh water
- first aid kit

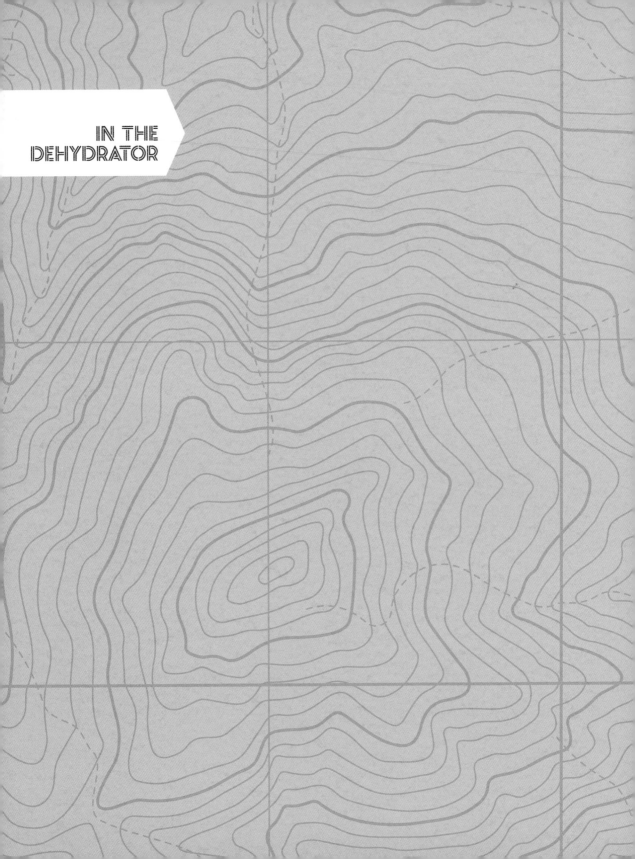

IN THE DEHYDRATOR

IN THE DEHYDRATOR

A dehydrator is an essential tool in your arsenal for making lightweight, affordable, easy-to-prepare, and 100 percent homemade meals and snacks. Not only can you control the amount of sodium and sugar going into your meals, but you can also dine confidently knowing you aren't consuming the unpronounceable preservatives that are often added to keep a product shelf-stable. Sure, there are a few things to learn when you're just starting out, and, yes, dehydrating times are lengthy, but the great news is that the process is almost completely hands-off for most foods. I promise you, with some easy home prep and a bit of planning, taking your own dehydrated meals and snacks into the backcountry is a whole lot easier than you think.

Need more convincing? Here are a few more great reasons to own a dehydrator:

- **Cost-effective.** You'll spend money up front purchasing a dehydrator, but what you make up in food-cost savings in the long run will far outweigh the price tag. For example, one pound of fresh mushrooms will yield about 3 ounces dehydrated—that may not sound like much, but considering that dried mushrooms are often sold in ½ ounce packages at more than $5 a pop, that 3 ounces from your dehydrator is a lot of bang (er, mushroom) for your buck.
- **Cuts down on food waste.** You can dehydrate almost anything. Unexpected bounty from your vegetable garden or food-share box? Overly generous yield from your pear tree? With a dehydrator, you can preserve what you're unable to eat fresh, enjoying it later, when it is out of season.
- **Ideal for drying food.** Dehydrators cook at temperatures between 95°F and 170°F, much lower than a standard oven, and circulate air to evenly dry food. And because the dehydrator does not cook at a high temperature, it's very hard to over-dry most foods, making it nearly foolproof.
- **Empowering.** Some recipes call for ingredients that are difficult to find dried or dehydrated. If you do find them, they are often expensive or need to be special ordered. Having a dehydrator puts the power in your hands, making it possible to create exactly what you want, when you want it.

CHOOSING A DEHYDRATOR

Dehydrators run the gamut from inexpensive, no-frills models to high-end commercial types that cost hundreds of dollars. If you're mainly looking to make snacks, jerky, and backpacking meals, your best bet lies somewhere in the middle of those extremes. While models will vary, here are some features worth paying special attention to:

- **Temperature.** You'll want the temperature to go up to at least 160°F, the minimum temperature needed to make jerky.
- **Automatic timer.** This helpful feature will automatically shut off the dehydrator after it's reached the end of its set cooking time, allowing you to mostly set it and forget it.
- **Vertical versus horizontal.** Vertical units have a fan at the bottom that circulates air and heat up toward stacked trays, while horizontal units have a fan in the back and food is loaded onto trays from the side. Most commercial-grade dehydrators are horizontal, but these tend to be larger, noisier, and more expensive. A decent vertical model will do the job, but know that the cheapest ones will likely require you to rotate the trays during drying since they don't heat as evenly.
- **Accessories.** While totally optional, some nice-to-haves include mesh trays for drying small ingredients and trays specifically made for making fruit leather. If you want to skip these, a piece of parchment paper will work just fine in most cases.

DEHYDRATING TIPS AND TRICKS

- **Keep a clean workspace.** If you're making beef jerky, for example, avoid cross contamination by sanitizing your hands, knife, and cutting board. Always thaw frozen meats in the refrigerator and keep refrigerated until ready to use.
- **Avoid mixing sweet and savory ingredients.** Dehydrate one type of food at a time to keep food smells where they belong.
- **Watch your spacing.** Don't overlap food on the trays and leave enough room between pieces to allow air to circulate.
- **Cut food to the same size and thickness for even drying.** Consider purchasing a mandoline slicer for thin, uniform slices every time (see p. 21).

- **Drying times are approximate.** And those times can fluctuate wildly depending on the food, the season, and your home environment, so use what's listed in this book as a starting point only.
- **Expiration dates vary.** Once dehydrated food has cooled completely, store in a resealable plastic bag, glass canning jar, or other airtight container. Fruits can be safely stored at room temperature for up to a year, vegetables for six months, jerky for two months, and fruit leather for one month. These times can be extended by using a vacuum sealer (see p. 20). Always label and date dried foods to keep track of their freshness.

DEHYDRATED FRUIT

The dehydrating process for fruit is pretty much the same no matter what type you choose (the dehydrator temperature remains the same); however, the time will vary greatly depending on the fruit, your dehydrator, and the temperature and humidity of your home. Times listed here are a good start, but you'll want to keep an eye on your fruit to check for when it's actually done. Aim for a chewy, pliable texture with no tackiness but not so tough that it's hard to eat. Some fruits, such as apples or bananas, oxidize and turn brown after they've been cut. While harmless, it's unappetizing to look at, and there's a simple solution to retain the color: as you're cutting the fruit, toss the slices into a bowl with equal parts lemon juice and water, then drain before dehydrating.

YIELDS	EQUIPMENT
2 pounds fruit makes about 1 cup dehydrated	Dehydrator

2 pounds fruit, cut into ¼-inch-thick slices

Home prep: Preheat dehydrator to 135°F. Wash fruit, then cut into ¼-inch slices. Spread onto dehydrating racks without any pieces overlapping. Dehydrate according to the times listed below, checking occasionally for doneness.

Fruit	Drying time (approximate)	Fruit	Drying time (approximate)
bananas	6–8 hours	kiwi	8–10 hours
strawberries	6–8 hours	apples	8–10 hours
mangoes	8–10 hours	apricots	10–12 hours
pears	8–10 hours	peaches	10–12 hours

SWEET FRUIT LEATHERS

You can make fruit leather with just about any type of fruit (fresh or frozen) that's been peeled, pitted, and pureed in a food processor or blender. If you're using fruit that is low in pectin, such as strawberries, rhubarb, or raspberries, mixing it with a higher pectin fruit, such as apples, blueberries, grapes, pineapples, or peaches, will create more pliable rolls. Alternatively, store-bought applesauce can be added to up the amount of pectin.

Some dehydrators have trays dedicated to fruit leather, but if not, a parchment-lined tray works well too. How much you make at one time depends on the size of your dehydrator, but a good rule of thumb is to use about 1 cup of fruit puree per tray. It also tends to thin out around the edges, so leave a slightly thicker layer on the sides for more even results. To make it easier to remove from the tray or parchment paper, peel the fruit leather off while it's still warm, about 15 minutes after taking it out of the dehydrator. Then let it cool completely before storing.

YIELDS	EQUIPMENT
1 cup fruit puree makes 1 roll	Dehydrator Blender or food processor

1 cup fruit puree per roll

Home prep: Puree fruit, then spread evenly in a ¼-inch-thick layer on the fruit leather tray for your dehydrator or on a piece of parchment paper. Dehydrate at 135°F until the surface is no longer wet or tacky, about 4–6 hours. Store in an airtight container.

TOMATO LEATHER (DEHYDRATED TOMATO SAUCE)

You can make leather out of just about any fruit, including tomatoes. Tomato leather is particularly handy for backpacking, as the easy-to-carry leather transforms into tomato sauce to use in a variety of soups, stews, and pasta dishes.

YIELDS	EQUIPMENT
Makes 2 rolls, or about 4 cups reconstituted tomato sauce	Dehydrator

1 15-ounce can crushed tomatoes
1 6-ounce can tomato paste

Home prep: Mix crushed tomatoes and paste together in a small saucepan. Simmer over medium heat until slightly thickened, about 10 minutes. Let cool slightly, then spread evenly in a ¼-inch-thick layer on the fruit leather tray for your dehydrator or on a piece of parchment paper. Dehydrate at 135°F until the surface is no longer wet or tacky, about 6 hours. Store in an airtight container.

At camp: Reconstitute in 3–4 cups boiling water to make sauce, or use according to your recipe's directions, stirring frequently to dissolve.

DEHYDRATED MUSHROOMS

Dehydrating mushrooms concentrates their flavor, making them perfect for adding a hit of savory depth to soups, stews, and sauces. Any variety of mushroom will work, as long as they're thinly sliced. One pound of fresh mushrooms yields about 3 ounces dried.

YIELDS		EQUIPMENT
1 pound fresh makes 3 ounces		Dehydrator

1 pound fresh mushrooms, rinsed and cut into ¼-inch-thick slices

Home prep: Dehydrate at 130°F for 6–8 hours, or until mushrooms are completely dry. Store in an airtight container.

At camp: To rehydrate, simply soak in water for 20 minutes (if you're making soup, retain the soaking water—it's infused with mushroom flavor).

DEHYDRATED FROZEN MIXED VEGETABLES

The beauty of dehydrating frozen soup vegetables such as corn, peas, and carrots is that they've already been blanched, saving you a step. Even better, there's no need to thaw them before dehydrating. Corn, peas, and carrots can be dehydrated at the same time (such as for Mushroom and Quinoa Soup, p. 119) or separately (as for Backcountry Chowder, p. 115, or Black Bean and Sweet Potato Chili, p. 135).

YIELDS	EQUIPMENT
1 cup frozen vegetables makes ½ cup dehydrated	Dehydrator

1 cup frozen mixed vegetables such as corn, peas, and carrots

Home prep: Spread frozen vegetables evenly on parchment-lined dehydrator trays and dehydrate at 135°F for 8–10 hours, or until completely dry (vegetables will be hard and crunchy). Store in an airtight container.

At camp: Soak vegetables in water for 15–20 minutes to speed up the rehydrating process, or simmer for 10–15 minutes (or use according to recipe directions).

DEHYDRATED BEANS

Canned beans of any variety dehydrate well, making them ideal additions to backpacking meals such as soups and stews. One 15-ounce can of beans will yield about a cup of dehydrated beans. The quantity depends on how much you want to make and the size of your dehydrator, but dehydrated beans keep well, so you might as well fill up your dehydrator and store the extra beans in an airtight container.

YIELDS	EQUIPMENT
1 15-ounce can makes 1 cup dehydrated	Dehydrator

1 15-ounce can beans, drained and rinsed

Home prep: Drain beans and rinse well in a colander and gently pat dry with a paper towel. Spread evenly onto parchment-lined dehydrator trays and dehydrate at 145°F for 6–8 hours, or until beans are completely dry. Store in an airtight container.

At camp: Soak beans for 15–20 minutes in water before cooking to help speed up the rehydration process, or use according to your recipe's directions.

DEHYDRATED GROUND MEAT

This recipe calls for ground beef, but feel free to experiment with other lean proteins. Ground bison and turkey are great substitutes that are naturally lean. As with jerky, fat is your enemy when it comes to drying meat, so be sure to start with lean beef (93 percent lean) and render as much as you can during the cooking process. The beef will be hard when completely dried and shouldn't be greasy.

YIELDS	EQUIPMENT
1 pound fresh makes 3 cups dehydrated	Dehydrator

1 pound 93 percent lean ground beef (or other lean protein)
Salt and pepper

Home prep: Cook beef in a skillet over medium heat, seasoning lightly with salt and pepper and breaking up into small pieces, until browned and any liquid has evaporated, 10–15 minutes. Remove from heat and scoop onto a paper towel–lined plate. Blot with paper towels to remove as much grease as you can.

Dehydrate at 155–160°F for 6–8 hours, or until completely dry. Store in an airtight container for up to two weeks at room temperature.

At camp: To rehydrate, put meat in a pot with just enough water to cover it, bring to a boil, then reduce heat and simmer for 10–15 minutes.

BEEF JERKY

Put your own spin on this classic trail snack by choosing the flavors yourself, or try one of the marinades on p. 49.

YIELDS	EQUIPMENT
1 pound fresh beef makes ⅓–½ pound jerky	Dehydrator

1 pound lean beef of your choice

Choosing the right cut: Fat is your enemy when it comes to preserving meat, so be sure to choose a lean cut of meat. Eye of round, flank steak, and the bottom/top round will all work well. Game meats such as elk, venison, and bison are naturally lean, making them good options for jerky as well.

Home prep: Start by putting the meat in the freezer for 30 minutes to make it easier to cut thin slices. Cut into slices between ⅛- and ¼-inch thick. For more tender jerky, cut across the grain, and if you prefer chewier bites, cut along the grain. Choose your marinade, then marinate in the refrigerator overnight.

The next day, preheat your dehydrator to 160–165°F. Remove the meat from the marinade and pat completely dry with paper towels. Place jerky strips on dehydrator racks, leaving space between each piece.

Dehydrating time can vary wildly, so pick a day when you'll be able to check on it throughout the process. Begin checking after about 4 hours, but the process can take up to 8 hours. Before testing a piece, let it sit at room temperature for a few minutes. You're looking for jerky that is well dried, with no sticky or wet spots on the surface, yet still pliable. When you bend it, it should crack slightly without breaking.

According to the National Center for Home Food Preservation, homemade beef jerky can be stored in a sealed container at room temperature for two weeks, and longer if you vacuum seal, refrigerate, or freeze whatever you don't plan on using within that time.

TOFU JERKY

Tofu jerky offers a quick, easy way to down some needed protein on the trail. Be sure to use the non-silken variety, as the silken type won't have a classic jerky-like chew. Marinating the tofu in a flat-bottomed glass or plastic container, rather than a bowl or plastic bag, helps keep the slices intact before going into the dehydrator. Use the marinade below, or try using one of the jerky marinades on p. 49.

YIELDS		EQUIPMENT
Makes ⅓–½ pound jerky		Dehydrator

1 block firm or extra-firm tofu

MARINADE
3 tablespoons Worcestershire sauce
1 tablespoon honey
1 tablespoon sriracha
2 tablespoons soy sauce
1 tablespoon water
1 teaspoon ground pepper

Home prep: Press tofu by cutting the block into 4 equally thick slices. Place on a paper towel–lined baking sheet, cover with paper towels, followed by a cutting board with a weight on top (a cast-iron pan or thick cookbook works well). Let sit for 30 minutes to drain out any liquid. Meanwhile, combine remaining ingredients (or marinade of choice, p. 49).

When tofu is pressed, cut into thin slices, no more than ¼-inch thick. Arrange slices in a container and add marinade, making sure all slices are well coated. Refrigerate and marinate overnight.

Remove tofu from the marinade and pat dry with a paper towel. Dehydrate at 140°F for 5–6 hours, or until tofu is dry but still chewy. Store in an airtight container for up to 1 month.

Jerky Marinades

Try a marinade recipe below, or create your own using ingredients you already have on hand. Jerky marinades are extremely forgiving as long as you hit the right notes of sweet, sour, salty, savory, and spicy.

YIELDS	DIETARY NOTES
Makes marinade for 1 pound of meat (before dehydrating)	Dairy-free

PINEAPPLE HOISIN

½ cup pineapple juice

½ cup hoisin sauce

2 tablespoons fish sauce

2 tablespoons sambal oelek or sriracha

CAROLINA BARBECUE

½ cup yellow mustard

¼ cup apple cider vinegar

¼ cup maple syrup

2 tablespoons soy sauce

1 tablespoon liquid smoke

1 tablespoon pepper

CHIPOTLE LIME

½ cup freshly squeezed lime juice (about 6 limes)

¼ cup honey

¼ cup chopped chipotle chiles in adobo, seeds removed

2 tablespoons soy sauce

MISO CURRY

¼ cup miso

¼ cup rice vinegar

2 tablespoons red curry paste

2 tablespoons fish sauce

2 tablespoons sambal oelek or sriracha

2 tablespoons honey

¼ cup water

Here are a few ideas that you can mix and match:

Sweet: maple syrup, honey, brown sugar, molasses, agave syrup

Sour: vinegars, citrus juice, tamarind paste, pickle juice, pineapple juice

Salty: fish sauce, soy sauce, miso

Savory: Worcestershire sauce, liquid smoke, ketchup, tomato paste, fish sauce

Spicy: hot sauce, gochujang, harissa, sambal oelek, chile flakes, black pepper, chile powder, curry powder, canned chipotle chiles

BREAKFAST

BREAKFAST

Note: 🥾 = backpacking-friendly recipes

OVERNIGHT OATS

As simple recipes go, this one ranks high. The only cooking equipment you need is an empty water bottle—no stove required. Just mix the ingredients before you go to bed, and let the water do the work for you. After trying this creamy, no-cook oatmeal, you may never go back to the instant packets again.

YIELDS	CAMPING STYLE	EQUIPMENT	DIETARY NOTES
Serves 2	Backcountry 🚶	Water bottle	Vegetarian Gluten-free Dairy-free ⊘ 🌾 🥛

1 cup rolled oats
½ cup dried blueberries
½ cup slivered almonds
¼ cup coconut milk powder
2 tablespoons chia seeds
2 tablespoons almond butter
1 tablespoon maple syrup or honey
1½ cups cold water
Optional garnish: chopped fresh fruit

Home prep: Combine oats, blueberries, almonds, coconut milk powder, and chia seeds in a resealable bag. Pack almond butter and sweetener separately.

At camp: In an empty water bottle or other container, combine all ingredients with water. Let sit at least 4 hours and up to overnight, then enjoy as is or add chopped fresh fruit.

HOW TO MAKE COWBOY COFFEE

Practically speaking, there isn't much more to making cowboy coffee than throwing grounds into hot water. However, there are a few smart measures you can take to make it coffee that's actually worth drinking (or foregoing instant coffee for). Spoiler alert: to cut down on the bitterness, this recipe gets a hand from an unexpected ingredient—salt! Here's the scoop you need to know to make a worthy cup of coffee at camp without any fancy tools:

The grounds: Grind them as coarse as your grinder will allow. This will make it easier to filter out the grounds and keep your coffee from becoming too gritty.

The ratio: You could measure out an exact ratio of water to grounds with a scale, but this is cowboy coffee, so it's perfectly okay to eyeball it. About 2 heaping tablespoons of coarsely ground coffee per cup of water will make a sufficiently strong pot.

The water: The hotter the water, the more bitter the coffee, so take care not to boil it once coffee and water are combined. Instead, bring a pot of water to a boil, then remove it from the heat, add your grounds, stir, cover, and let it brew for about 5 minutes before straining.

The salt: Yes, salt—but you need just a pinch, added when you mix the grounds with the water. Much more than that could make your coffee undrinkable, but a small amount helps neutralize some of the bitterness and enhances some of the sweetness and other nutty, toasty flavors.

The straining: If you don't have a pot with holes small enough to strain the grounds, pour it through a clean bandana or other piece of cloth. Or, if you don't mind a few grounds ending up in your cup, you can simply let the coffee sit long enough for the grounds to settle, then carefully pour it into your cup.

PANCAKES

Warm, stick-to-your-ribs pancakes are a great way to launch into a day of adventure. Buttermilk powder and a single-serving cup/packet of applesauce (in place of an egg) make this recipe backpacking-friendly.

YIELDS	CAMPING STYLE	EQUIPMENT	DIETARY NOTES
Serves 2	Backcountry 🏃	Nonstick or cast-iron skillet Two-burner or backpacking stove	Vegetarian

1 cup all-purpose flour
¼ cup buttermilk powder
1 tablespoon sugar
1 teaspoon baking powder
½ teaspoon baking soda
¼ teaspoon salt
¼ cup applesauce
1 cup water
Vegetable oil, for cooking
Maple syrup, for serving

Home prep: Combine dry ingredients. Pack applesauce, oil, and syrup separately in resealable plastic bags or other leak-proof containers.

At camp: Combine dry ingredients with applesauce and water, then mix until a lumpy batter is formed (avoid overmixing). Heat oil in a skillet over medium heat, then pour in batter about ¼ cup at a time. Cook until air bubbles form on the surface, then flip and cook until batter is set, about 1 minute per side. Repeat with remaining batter, then serve with maple syrup.

BANNOCK BISCUITS

Bannock bread has been a campfire staple for hundreds of years, with roots dating back to pre-contact Indigenous peoples in North America. Try these biscuits with Bacon Gravy (p. 62) or Mushroom Gravy (p. 65), or whip up a batch in the morning to use for sandwiches and snacks throughout the day.

YIELDS	CAMPING STYLE	EQUIPMENT	DIETARY NOTES
Makes 8–10 biscuits	Backcountry 🚶	Cast-iron or lightweight backpacking skillet Two-burner or backpacking stove	Vegetarian 🍃

1 cup all-purpose flour
2 teaspoons baking powder
2 tablespoons milk powder
1 teaspoon salt
½–¾ cup water
2 tablespoons vegetable oil

Home prep: Mix dry ingredients together in a gallon-size zip-top bag (this will be your mixing vessel in camp). Pack other ingredients separately.

At camp: Add water, a little bit at a time, to dry ingredients and mix until smooth, thick batter has formed. Heat oil in a skillet over medium-low heat and drop batter, about ¼ cup at a time, into separate lumps in the skillet. Cook until the bottom is lightly browned, about 2 minutes, then flip. Continue to cook until the other side is browned and a toothpick or fork stuck into the center comes out clean, about another 2 minutes. Repeat with remaining batter.

HOW TO MAKE A ROUX

When you come across a recipe that calls for making a roux, don't fret that it's an overly complicated French technique and run away. At its core, a roux is simply equal parts fat and flour, cooked together to use for thickening stews and sauces. It's the base for many recipes, from Creole and Cajun dishes to macaroni and cheese. How long it needs to cook depends on the dish; light roux is good for when you just need to cook the raw taste out of the flour to use as a thickener without adding any particular flavors of its own. For some recipes, such as gumbo, a dark roux is a defining characteristic of the dish, cooked until the flour has darkened and developed a rich, nutty flavor. While making roux does require your undivided attention, the process and ingredients are simple. Here are a few tips to keep you on the right track:

- **Watch it closely.** Roux can go from done to scorched in a surprisingly short period of time.
- **Stir it constantly.** Keep the mixture moving to prevent it from burning and so the flour darkens evenly. The best method is to use a whisk in a cast-iron skillet.
- **Go easy on the burner.** Medium heat is about as high as you want to go.
- **Choose your fat wisely.** Any fat will do, but each will have its own strengths and weaknesses. Butter is good for a light roux that isn't cooked for longer than a few minutes, but for a dark roux, it can burn easily. For a dark roux, vegetable oil or rendered animal fats can stand up to longer cooking times but impart a stronger flavor to the finished dish (which can be good or bad, depending on your goal).

- **Light roux is best for thickening.** Dark roux loses some of its thickening capability as it cooks. Light roux is usually ready in less than five minutes.
- **Dark roux needs your attention.** While more flavorful and complex than light roux, dark roux requires more care and time. For a true dark roux, you will need to cook and stir it constantly until it's the color of milk chocolate. Over a medium or low burner, this can take 30 to 45 minutes. You can speed up the process by using higher heat, but be careful not to scorch it, which will turn it bitter. If you go this route, use a fat or oil with a higher smoke point, such as grapeseed oil or sunflower oil.
- **Be patient.** The time and care are well worth it. If you've done it right, you'll be surprised by how much flavor and complexity you can coax out of two of the most basic ingredients in your pantry.

BACON GRAVY

This flavorful, homestyle gravy makes the perfect partner for freshly made Bannock Biscuits (p. 58) or another favorite biscuit.

YIELDS	CAMPING STYLE	EQUIPMENT
Serves 2–3	Frontcountry 🚗	Cast-iron skillet Two-burner stove

3 strips bacon
2 tablespoons all-purpose flour
2 cups milk (fresh or reconstituted from milk powder)
Salt and pepper, to taste
Biscuits and Louisiana-style hot sauce, for serving

Home prep: Pack all ingredients separately.

At camp: Heat bacon in a skillet over medium-low heat, cooking slowly to render fat, until bacon is crispy and well-done. Remove bacon, let cool slightly, and crush into small pieces. Set aside, and reserve 2 tablespoons of the grease in the skillet.

Increase heat to medium and add flour, stirring frequently (this flour-fat mixture is called a roux; see p. 60). Continue to cook roux until lightly browned, stirring constantly to prevent burning, 2–3 minutes.

Add milk in a slow, steady stream while continuing to stir. Add crushed bacon, then bring to a boil, reduce heat and simmer until gravy has thickened, 5–10 minutes. Season with salt and pepper and serve over biscuits, along with extra pepper and Louisiana-style hot sauce.

MUSHROOM GRAVY

Dehydrated mushrooms (p. 43) swapped in for meat make this diner-classic recipe backpacking-friendly. Serve over your favorite biscuits, or make your own Bannock Biscuits (p. 58) in camp.

YIELDS	CAMPING STYLE	EQUIPMENT	DIETARY NOTES
Serves 2–3	Backcountry	Lightweight backpacking cook set	Vegetarian
		Backpacking stove	
		Dehydrator	

⅔ cup milk powder (or 2 cups reconstituted milk)
1 bouillon cube
2 cups water
¾ ounce dehydrated mushrooms (see recipe, p. 43)
2 tablespoons coconut oil
2 tablespoons all-purpose flour
Salt and pepper, to taste
Biscuits and Louisiana-style hot sauce, for serving

Home prep: Pack all ingredients separately.

At camp: In a bowl, stir milk powder and bouillon cube into 2 cups water (it's all right if the bouillon cube isn't dissolved). Tear mushrooms into small pieces and add to the mixture, soaking them until they're rehydrated, about 20 minutes.

When mushrooms are soft, make a roux by heating oil in a pot over medium and then adding flour, stirring frequently (see p. 60). Continue to cook the roux until lightly browned, stirring constantly to prevent burning, about 2–3 minutes.

Add mushroom mixture in a slow, steady stream while continuing to stir. Bring to a boil, reduce heat, and simmer until gravy has thickened, 5–10 minutes. Season with salt and pepper and serve over biscuits, along with extra pepper and Louisiana-style hot sauce.

COFFEE AND BANANA BREAKFAST BARS

In case you're wondering if eating coffee grounds does anything for your caffeine intake, the answer is yes. Your body absorbs the caffeine quickly when consumed this way, so tread lightly with these—each bar contains about the same amount of caffeine as one cup of coffee.

YIELDS	CAMPING STYLE	DIETARY NOTES
Makes 9 bars	Backcountry 🚶	Vegetarian Gluten-free Dairy-free

2 ripe bananas
1½ cups rolled oats
½ cup sliced almonds, lightly crushed
¼ cup ground coffee
¼ cup shredded coconut
⅓ cup honey
1 teaspoon vanilla extract
½ teaspoon salt

Home prep: Preheat oven to 350°F. Mash bananas in a large bowl, then add remaining ingredients and press into a greased 8×8-inch baking dish. Bake until oats are lightly browned on top, 25–30 minutes. Cool completely, then cut into 9 squares. Wrap in plastic wrap or store in a resealable plastic bag for up to 1 week.

Breakfast

DILL AND JUNIPER–CURED SALMON GRAVLAX WITH MUSTARD SAUCE

Gravlax, aka lox, is unsmoked, cured fish, so you'll want to seek out the freshest fish possible (see p. 69). Use it on a bagel with cream cheese and capers for a quick, high-protein breakfast, or serve it the traditional Scandinavian way on pumpernickel with mustard sauce for a fancy campsite brunch.

YIELDS	CAMPING STYLE	DIETARY NOTES
Serves 6	Frontcountry	Gluten-free (without Mustard Sauce)
	🚗	Dairy-free

1 pound salmon, skin on, cut from
    the center of the fillet
2 tablespoons salt
2 tablespoons sugar
2 tablespoons gin or aquavit, optional
1 tablespoon juniper berries, lightly
    crushed

1 bunch fresh dill, chopped
Optional garnishes: cream cheese,
    capers, sliced red onions,
    chopped fresh dill, mustard sauce
    (recipe follows, p. 70)
Bagels or pumpernickel slices,
    for serving

Home prep: Rinse salmon under cold water and pat dry with a paper towel. Mix salt and sugar together in a small bowl. Drizzle gin over salmon (if desired), then sprinkle salt and sugar mixture generously over both sides of fish, ensuring it is well coated. Spread juniper berries and dill over the flesh side, then wrap in plastic. Place in a shallow baking dish, skin side up, then place another flat-bottomed dish with a few weights on top to press down firmly and evenly on the salmon. Refrigerate 24 hours, then flip so salmon is skin side down, replace weights, and refrigerate another 24 hours. After 48 hours, remove salmon from plastic wrap and wipe off any remaining cure with a paper towel (rinsing under water is not necessary). Now your salmon is cured and ready to eat.

At camp: Slice salmon into thin slices (a sharp knife is crucial for getting clean slices) at a 45-degree angle. Cured salmon can be kept for up to 5 days in the refrigerator or well-tended cooler, wrapped tightly in plastic wrap. Garnish, and serve with pumpernickel slices or bagels, if desired.

NOTE ON RAW FISH

Many gravlax recipes call for "sushi-grade" fish, but that term doesn't actually mean anything. As opposed to meats that are labeled for quality, such as "prime" or "choice" beef, terms that are ascribed by the US Department of Agriculture, there is no governing body that labels fish as such. Fishmongers may use the term as they see fit, and you simply have to take their word for it. So how do you know if what you're eating is safe? Here are a few ways to mitigate the risk of eating raw fish:

- Buy from a trusted source, and ask the fishmonger if they would recommend a fillet for eating raw.
- Use farmed Atlantic salmon; wild-caught salmon are more susceptible to worms and parasites. Norwegian and Scottish farmed salmon in particular rank high in sustainability and in following best aquaculture practices.
- Keep your fish cold at all times (below 40°F).
- Keep your prep area and utensils clean and sanitized.
- Some recipes call for freezing your fish in order to kill parasites, but this works only if your freezer can be set to -4°F or below (0°F is the standard for home freezers) and the fish stays frozen for at least seven days, according to the FDA.
- If you have doubts about the freshness of your fish or the trustworthiness of your source, skip using it for any raw preparation.

Mustard Sauce

Serve this alongside gravlax on slices of rye or pumpernickel bread.

YIELDS	DIETARY NOTES
Makes ½ cup	Vegetarian
	Dairy-free
	⊘ ⊠

3 tablespoons Dijon mustard
3 tablespoons apple cider vinegar
1 tablespoon honey
¼ cup extra-virgin olive oil
3 tablespoons fresh dill, chopped

Home prep: In a medium bowl, whisk together mustard, vinegar, and honey. Gradually add oil in a steady stream, whisking constantly, until sauce is smooth and emulsified. Stir in dill, then store in a cooler or refrigerator until ready to use. (Note: Letting it sit for a few hours before using helps flavors come together.)

SKILLET FRITTATA, FOUR WAYS

Not as fussy as an omelet, but a step up from a simple scramble, frittatas borrow a few tricks from both and combine them into one tidy package. Once you have the technique down, this recipe is a blank canvas. It's based on using an 8-inch skillet, which can accommodate 4–6 eggs (2–3 servings), but don't be afraid to add more eggs and other ingredients than the recipe calls for. You can scale up with a larger skillet, but the flip will be slightly more complicated.

(Note: Don't attempt this without a nonstick skillet or a *very* well-seasoned cast-iron pan.)

YIELDS	CAMPING STYLE	EQUIPMENT	DIETARY NOTES
Serves 2–3	Frontcountry 🚗	Nonstick skillet Two-burner or backpacking stove	Vegetarian Gluten-free ∅ 🌾

GREEK-STYLE

4 large eggs
½ teaspoon salt
½ teaspoon pepper
¼ cup sliced zucchini
⅓ cup crumbled feta cheese
¼ cup Kalamata olives, roughly chopped
½ tablespoon olive oil

Home prep: If you have a cooler at your disposal, nearly all prep can be done at home. Combine eggs, salt, and pepper in a Mason jar, shaking well to beat eggs. Sauté zucchini (or any other fillings that need to be cooked beforehand) over medium-high heat until lightly browned but not mushy, about 5 minutes. Cool, then combine with remaining ingredients in a jar, except olive oil, and you're ready to cook.

At camp: Heat oil over medium-low heat. Add egg mixture, scraping sides toward the center of the pan and swirling to evenly cook curds. Continue to cook gently until eggs are mostly set on the surface.

Remove the pan from the burner and put a plate on top of the pan. Flip over, then slide the frittata off the plate and back into the pan (this is where a nonstick pan is essential). Cook a few more minutes, just until the bottom is set. Slice and serve.

OTHER COMBOS

The formula is always the same: prepare fillings, slowly cook eggs, then flip. Here are some other classic combinations, but feel free to bushwhack on your own. Aim for about a cup of prepared fillings for a 4-egg frittata, or scale up as needed.

Ranchero: black beans, chorizo, corn tortilla strips, Cotija cheese, topped with salsa

Denver: diced hard salami, sautéed green bell peppers, cheddar cheese

Goat: chèvre, cooked bacon, chopped dates

HUEVOS RANCHEROS

Huevos rancheros doesn't require much more thought than your standard egg breakfast, but with a few extra steps and ingredients, it becomes so much more. This tasty crowd-pleaser is simple enough for a quick meal and easy to scale up or scale down depending on the size of your group.

YIELDS	CAMPING STYLE	EQUIPMENT	DIETARY NOTES
Serves 4	Frontcountry 🚗	Cast-iron skillet Two-burner stove Aluminum foil	Vegetarian Gluten-free ⊘🌿

½ teaspoon ground cumin
½ teaspoon ground coriander
1 15-ounce can black beans
1 teaspoon oil
4 corn tortillas
6–8 eggs
1 cup crumbled cheese, such as feta or Cotija
1 cup salsa
Salt and pepper, to taste
Optional garnishes: hot sauce, lime wedges, sour cream,
    avocado, chopped cilantro, pickled jalapeños

Home prep: Combine cumin and coriander, and pack in a sealed container or bag. Pack other ingredients separately.

At camp: Combine beans and spices in a pot, bring to a boil, cover, then simmer for 5 minutes. Remove from heat and set aside.

While beans cook, heat 1 teaspoon of oil in a skillet over medium-high heat. Cook tortillas one at a time until lightly crisped but still pliable, about 30 seconds per side. Wrap in foil and keep warm until ready to serve. Prepare desired garnishes.

When beans, tortillas, and garnishes are ready to serve, scramble eggs or make to order. Place a tortilla on each plate, top with beans, eggs, cheese, salsa, and garnishes.

SHAKSHUKA

This savory Middle Eastern stew comes together quickly for a hearty meal. Eggs are poached in tomato sauce until the whites are just set—or until the yolks aren't runny, if you prefer. You can alter the number of eggs depending on how many servings you want; a 10-inch skillet will accommodate up to 6 eggs. If you can't find Aleppo pepper and Za'atar, cayenne or ground thyme, respectively, can be substituted.

YIELDS	CAMPING STYLE	EQUIPMENT	DIETARY NOTES
Serves 2–4	Frontcountry 🚗	Cast-iron skillet Two-burner stove	Vegetarian Gluten-free Dairy-free (without feta)

1 onion, thinly sliced
1 red bell pepper, thinly sliced
1 tablespoon smoked paprika
1 tablespoon Za'atar (or ground thyme)
1 teaspoon ground cumin
½ teaspoon Aleppo pepper (or cayenne)
1 bay leaf
¼ cup olive oil

Salt and pepper, to taste
4 garlic cloves, roughly chopped
1 28-ounce can whole peeled tomatoes
4–6 eggs
½ cup crumbled feta cheese
¼ cup chopped cilantro
Naan or bread, for serving

Home prep: Mix sliced onion and bell pepper together in a zip-top bag or other container. Mix paprika, Za'atar, cumin, Aleppo pepper, and bay leaf together in a separate container. Pack other ingredients separately.

At camp: Heat oil over medium-high heat until shimmering, then add onion and bell pepper. Season with salt and pepper, and sauté until browned and lightly charred, about 5 minutes. Lower heat to medium and add garlic and spice mixture. Stir to combine and cook until spices are fragrant, 1–2 minutes longer.

Add tomatoes, breaking them into smaller pieces with a spatula, stir to combine, then reduce heat to medium-low and simmer until sauce has thickened, 10–15 minutes, stirring occasionally.

Carefully crack eggs on top of tomato sauce and cook undisturbed until egg whites are just set, about 10 minutes, or longer if you want more well-done eggs (you can cover the pan with a lid or piece of foil to help whites set more quickly). Top with crumbled feta and chopped cilantro. Serve with naan, crusty bread, or enjoy simply on its own.

SNACKS, SIDES, AND LUNCHES

Note: 🥾 = backpacking-friendly recipes

BLUEBERRY AND ALMOND GRANOLA

This time-honored trail snack is endlessly adaptable, so as long as you keep the basic proportions the same, any nuts or berries of your choice can be swapped in for the blueberries or almonds. If you like your granola to stick together in clusters, be sure to press down firmly on the mixture during the last 15 minutes of baking.

YIELDS	CAMPING STYLE	DIETARY NOTES
Makes about 3 cups	Backcountry 🥾	Vegan Gluten-free Dairy-free

¼ cup vegetable oil
¼ cup maple syrup
1 teaspoon almond (or vanilla) extract
½ teaspoon salt
½ cup sliced almonds
1½ cups rolled oats
½ cup dried blueberries

Home prep: Preheat oven to 300°F. Mix oil, syrup, almond extract, and salt in a large bowl. Add almonds and oats, then mix thoroughly to combine. Spread out on a baking sheet in an even layer, then bake for 30 minutes, stirring halfway through, keeping the granola in a single layer. After 30 minutes, add dried blueberries, stir again, then press down firmly with a spatula (skip pressing if you don't want clusters). Bake until granola is golden brown, another 10–15 minutes. Let cool, then store in an airtight container for up to one month.

At camp: Eat as a tasty trail snack, or stir into oatmeal or yogurt for a quick and easy backcountry breakfast.

SMOKED OYSTERS WITH SERRANO MIGNONETTE OR CHIPOTLE COCKTAIL SAUCE

Rich in omega-3 fatty acids, high in protein, shelf-stable, affordable, and sustainable to boot, canned smoked oysters make a perfect snack or lunch in the backcountry. Better yet, here are two sauces you can pack into a small bottle or container to make these mollusks even tastier.

YIELDS	CAMPING STYLE	DIETARY NOTES
Each recipe makes enough for 2 cans of smoked oysters	Backcountry 🏃	Gluten-free Dairy-free

2 cans smoked oysters
Crackers or bread, for serving

SERRANO MIGNONETTE
1 small serrano pepper, stem and seeds removed, minced
1 small shallot, minced
3 tablespoons white wine vinegar
Pinch sugar
Pinch salt
Pinch pepper

CHIPOTLE COCKTAIL SAUCE
3 tablespoons ketchup
1 chipotle chile in adobo, seeds removed, minced
½ tablespoon prepared horseradish
Juice from ½ lemon

Home prep (same for either sauce recipe): Combine all sauce ingredients. Pack in a small squeeze bottle or other leak-proof container.

At camp: Drain oil from oyster tin and mix oysters with a tablespoon or two of sauce, reserving some for drizzling. Serve with crackers or bread.

KALE CHIPS

If you've ever asked yourself what is the easiest way to bring an entire bunch of kale into the backcountry and eat it all in one sitting, then here is your answer: kale chips. Crunchy, salty, tangy, and satisfying, these chips hit all the right notes without weighing you down.

YIELDS	CAMPING STYLE	DIETARY NOTES
Serves 3–4	Backcountry 🚶	Vegan Gluten-free Dairy-free

1 bunch curly kale
1 tablespoon olive oil
2 tablespoons malt or apple cider vinegar
Salt, to taste

Home prep: Preheat oven to 300°F. Meanwhile, wash kale, remove stems, and pat dry with paper towels. Tear into 2-inch pieces and toss into a bowl with oil and vinegar. Massage leaves to soften them, then spread onto a parchment-lined baking sheet in an even layer, making sure not to overlap pieces. Sprinkle with salt, then bake for 10 minutes. Remove from oven, flip kale pieces over (they won't be crisp yet, don't worry), and continue to bake 10–15 minutes longer, or until crispy. Let cool and store in an airtight container.

At camp: Eat as a snack on the go, or crush into pieces and sprinkle over an entree for an extra bit of veggies.

TOMATO SOUP

This soup calls for dehydrated tomato leather, which you'll find a recipe for in the dehydrator section. It's important to add the milk toward the end of cooking and temper it, or you run the risk of curdling it or having it scorch and stick to the bottom of the pot, leaving you with an unwelcome cleaning task.

YIELDS	CAMPING STYLE	EQUIPMENT	DIETARY NOTES
Serves 2–3	Backcountry 🥾	Lightweight cook set Backpacking stove Dehydrator	Vegetarian Gluten-free ⌀ 🌾

2 ounces tomato leather (about ¾ of the recipe in this book, p. 42)
2 tablespoons dried minced onion
3 bouillon cubes
1 tablespoon dried basil
1 teaspoon garlic powder
1 teaspoon sugar
1 teaspoon smoked paprika
Salt and pepper, to taste
⅓ cup milk powder
4 cups water, divided

Home prep: Combine all ingredients, except milk powder and water, in a zip-top bag or other container.

At camp: Mix milk powder with 1 cup water in a bowl, then set aside.

In a pot, combine 3 cups of water along with remaining ingredients. Bring to a boil, cover, reduce heat, and simmer until tomato leather has disintegrated and soup is cooked through, stirring occasionally, 7–10 minutes.

Add ½ cup of hot soup to the milk mixture in order to temper. Remove pot from heat, then add tempered milk mixture and stir to combine. Serve with crackers or Bannock Biscuits (p. 58), if desired.

SPAM MUSUBI

These handheld, nori-wrapped rice and SPAM snacks are a Japanese-Hawaiian mash-up that are affordable, portable, and easy to make. If you're planning on adding these to your regular rotation of snacks and lunches, it's worth spending $5 on a musubi mold. Otherwise, use the empty SPAM can to shape the rice.

YIELDS	CAMPING STYLE	EQUIPMENT	DIETARY NOTES
Makes 8 musubi snacks	Frontcountry 🚗	Musubi mold (or empty SPAM can)	Dairy-free

¼ cup soy sauce
¼ cup sugar
1 tablespoon Worcestershire sauce
1 tablespoon sriracha
1 can SPAM (low sodium, if available)
2 cups short-grain rice, cooked
2 tablespoons rice vinegar
1 teaspoon oil
4 sheets nori, cut in half

Home prep: Mix soy sauce, sugar, Worcestershire sauce, and sriracha together until sugar is dissolved. Cut SPAM into 8 slices, then toss with marinade, and marinate at least 30 minutes or up to overnight in the refrigerator. Meanwhile, cook rice, then mix with rice vinegar. Let cool slightly before assembling musubi.

Heat skillet over medium-high heat with a teaspoon of oil. Fry SPAM slices until browned on each side, 1–2 minutes per side. Set aside until ready to assemble.

To assemble musubi, place mold in the center of one of the halved sheets of nori. Put ¼ cup of rice into the mold, then pack down the rice. Add a slice of SPAM, remove mold, and fold nori over SPAM and rice, using fingers dipped in a small bowl of water to dampen nori sheet as you roll it over to seal edges. Repeat with remaining SPAM slices and rice. Wrap individual musubis in plastic wrap and store in a refrigerator or cooler.

At camp: Keep in a cooler until you're ready to hit the trail.

Snacks, Sides, and Lunches

SMOKED TROUT SPREAD

If you're lucky enough to land a cooler full of trout, there's no better way to stretch its shelf life than to smoke it, if you have the equipment. If not, a package of store-bought smoked trout or even salmon will still work great here.

YIELDS	CAMPING STYLE
Makes 2 cups	Frontcountry

¼ cup cream cheese
¾ cup Greek yogurt
1 tablespoon Dijon mustard
1 tablespoon lemon juice
½ tablespoon extra-virgin olive oil
10 ounces smoked trout, skin and bones removed (about 1 whole trout)
2 tablespoons fresh dill, chopped
2 tablespoons fresh chives, chopped
Salt and pepper, to taste
Crackers, bagels, or tortillas, for serving
Optional: capers, red onions, greens

Home prep: Mix cream cheese, yogurt, mustard, lemon juice, and oil together until creamy and well blended. Fold in trout and herbs, then salt and pepper to taste. Keep refrigerated or in a cooler.

At camp: Eat this with crackers while you're setting up camp for a quick snack or spread on a bagel or tortilla with capers, red onions, or greens for a light breakfast or lunch.

Snacks, Sides, and Lunches

TABBOULEH

This light, refreshing herb salad is easy to make ahead of time and is packed with fiber. The cucumber salting step isn't essential, but doing so will help keep the cucumbers crisp and the salad from becoming too watery as it sits.

YIELDS	CAMPING STYLE	DIETARY NOTES
Serves 4	Frontcountry 🚗	Vegan Dairy-free V⁰ 🥛

1 cup water
½ cup bulgur wheat
1 cucumber, finely diced
Salt, to taste
1 shallot, minced
1 bunch fresh mint, finely chopped (about ½ cup)
1 bunch fresh parsley, finely chopped (about 1½ cups)
1 pint cherry tomatoes, cut in half
⅓ cup olive oil
Juice from 2 lemons

Home prep: Bring water to a boil, then remove from heat and pour over bulgur. Let sit at least 10 minutes, or until bulgur is tender, then drain excess water and chill in the refrigerator.

Meanwhile, put diced cucumber in a colander placed inside of a bowl and sprinkle with salt. Let sit for 30 minutes to 1 hour, then pat with a paper towel to wipe off any excess salt.

When cucumbers and bulgur are prepared, combine with remaining ingredients. Adjust for salt, then store in the cooler or refrigerator until ready to serve.

At camp: Serve as a side salad or along with other small plates and snack foods for a tapas-style meal.

GUACAMOLE

Guacamole tends to elicit strong opinions, so I won't insist that my way is the best way (even if it is), but I will say that I prefer it chunky rather than smooth, heavy on the citrus, and always with plenty of cilantro. Consider this recipe as more of a starting point for experimenting—make it spicier by swapping the jalapeño for a serrano or habanero, or give it a sweet hint with a handful of pomegranate seeds.

YIELDS	CAMPING STYLE	DIETARY NOTES
Makes about 2 cups	Frontcountry 🚗	Vegan Gluten-free Dairy-free V 🥜 🥛

¼ cup red onion, finely minced
1 Roma tomato, finely chopped
1 jalapeño, stem and seeds removed, minced
⅓ cup chopped cilantro
Juice of 2 limes
Salt, to taste
4 small (or 3 large) avocados

Home prep: Car campers can make this ahead of time by combining onion, tomato, jalapeño, cilantro, lime juice, and a few pinches of salt in a medium bowl. Dice avocados into ½-inch chunks and gently fold into the rest of the ingredients, making sure to keep avocado chunks mostly intact (or mash into a smoother dip, if you prefer). Adjust for salt and citrus, then store in a cooler or refrigerator until needed (see note on keeping guac green, p. 97).

At camp: While you can fully prepare this in advance to make it a super-fast snack to feed hungry frontcountry campers, the ingredients and method are simple enough to prepare fresh in the backcountry if you have the time, interest, and space in your pack to keep the avocados intact.

HOW TO KEEP YOUR GUAC GREEN

Cut avocados will oxidize quickly, so to prevent them from becoming a brown, grayish mush, you'll want to counteract that process. If you're making guac ahead of time, then use this simple method to keep it fresh and green: Put the guacamole in the vessel you'll use to transport it to camp, smooth the surface with a spoon, and squeeze lime juice over that surface. Next, add a ½-inch layer of water on top. The reason this works is twofold. One, the acidity from the lime prevents the enzymes in the avocados from reacting with oxygen to slow browning, and two, the water creates an oxygen-proof barrier to the surface. Don't worry, your guac won't become watery—avocados are high in fat, keeping the water from penetrating the surface. When you're ready to serve, simply pour off the water on top.

CHARRED TOMATO SALSA

Don't be afraid to give the vegetables a good char under the broiler. If you want salsa verde, all you need to do is swap the tomatoes for husked tomatillos, or for a spicier salsa, swap the jalapeños for serranos.

YIELDS	CAMPING STYLE	DIETARY NOTES
Makes about 2 cups	Frontcountry 🚗	Vegan Gluten-free Dairy-free V⁰ 🐝 🥛

1 pound Roma tomatoes, halved lengthwise
1 red onion, halved lengthwise
4 garlic cloves, unpeeled
2 jalapeños, halved lengthwise, stem and seeds removed
½ cup chopped cilantro
Juice from 2 limes (about ¼ cup juice)
1 teaspoon salt
½ teaspoon sugar
Tortilla chips, for serving

Home prep: Preheat broiler to high. Put tomatoes and onion (cut side up) on a foil-lined baking sheet, along with garlic and jalapeños (skin side up). Broil until vegetables are blackened and well charred, 10–15 minutes. Let sit until cool enough to handle.

Peel garlic and remove blackened skin from jalapeños. Put all ingredients into a blender or food processor and blend until smooth. Adjust for salt, then store in a cooler or refrigerator until ready to use.

At camp: Serve with tortilla chips or use as a topping for Huevos Rancheros (p. 75) or Flank Steak Fajitas (p. 152).

DUTCH OVEN GREEN CHILE AND CHEESE CORNBREAD

Green chile and cheese are a classic combination, but this works as a base recipe for however you'd like to adjust to your own taste. You could add cooked corn in place of the green chiles or omit the cheese and chiles and double the amount of sugar for a sweeter cornbread. The batter can be made a day or two ahead of time and kept in a cooler or refrigerator, cutting down on prep time in camp. You can use canned green chiles or follow the directions for roasting green chiles yourself (p. 147).

YIELDS	CAMPING STYLE	EQUIPMENT	DIETARY NOTES
Serves 6–8	Frontcountry 🚗	Dutch oven Charcoal chimney starter (or hot campfire coals)	Vegetarian

2 eggs
¼ cup vegetable oil
1 cup buttermilk
2 tablespoons sugar
½ teaspoon salt
1½ cups medium-grind cornmeal

½ cup all-purpose flour
½ cup grated cheddar cheese
¼ cup diced green chiles
2 teaspoons baking powder
Vegetable oil, for greasing Dutch oven

Home prep: In a large bowl, beat eggs, then add oil, buttermilk, sugar, and salt, mixing to combine. Add remaining ingredients and mix to combine well. Keep batter in a cooler or refrigerator until ready to use.

At camp: Prepare ¾ of a chimney full of charcoal. When coals are lit, place ⅓ underneath Dutch oven on a fireproof surface and ⅔ on top of the lid. Let the oven preheat until hot, 5–7 minutes.

When the oven is hot, grease it with vegetable oil. Add batter and replace the lid, leaving it slightly cracked so steam can escape, allowing the top of the cornbread to brown. Bake until cornbread is risen and golden brown on top, 20–25 minutes. To test for doneness, insert a toothpick or knife into the center—when done, the toothpick should come out dry.

CAPONATA (SWEET-AND-SOUR EGGPLANT TOPPING)

Caponata is one of those recipes that actually improves if you make it in advance, making it a low-stress dish, as far as planning goes. This traditional sweet-and-sour Sicilian spread is based on eggplant, but beyond that feel free to substitute or add other ingredients to put your own spin on it.

YIELDS	CAMPING STYLE	EQUIPMENT	DIETARY NOTES
Makes 2 cups	Frontcountry 🚗	Cast-iron skillet	Vegan Gluten-free Dairy-free

½ cup pine nuts

⅓ cup extra-virgin olive oil, plus extra for sautéing

1 small eggplant (about 1 pound), cut into ½-inch dice

1 onion, diced

1 red bell pepper, diced

2 celery ribs, cut into ¼-inch pieces

1 pint cherry tomatoes

4 cloves garlic, minced

½ cup green or mixed pitted olives, roughly chopped

¼ cup raisins

2 tablespoons capers

1 tablespoon sugar

⅓ cup red wine vinegar

Salt and pepper, to taste

Bread or pita pocket, for serving

Home prep: Heat a large cast-iron skillet over medium heat (no oil) and add pine nuts. Toast, stirring frequently to keep them from burning, until lightly browned, about 1 minute. Remove from the pan and set aside.

Add olive oil to the skillet, then add eggplant and cook over medium heat until it has absorbed the oil and then released it again, about 10 minutes. Add onion, bell pepper, and celery, and continue to cook until browned and softened, about 10 minutes longer, adding a tablespoon or two of olive oil if needed. When the vegetables have softened and browned, add remaining ingredients and cook until cherry tomatoes have burst and mixture has become a thick, chunky sauce. Remove from heat and let cool to room temperature (or store in a cooler or refrigerator) until ready to serve.

At camp: Best eaten cold or at room temperature, this spread goes well on bread for an easy bruschetta or tucked into a pita pocket with a packet of tuna for a hearty lunch.

MARINATED WHITE BEANS

Like Caponata (p. 102), this make-ahead snack only improves as it sits and the flavors come together. Parsley and mint are a particularly tasty pairing, but just about any combination of herbs will work.

YIELDS	CAMPING STYLE	DIETARY NOTES
Makes 2 cups	Frontcountry 🚗	Vegan Gluten-free Dairy-free 🌱 🌾 🥛

1 15-ounce can cannellini (or other white) beans
⅓ cup chopped fresh parsley
2 tablespoons chopped fresh mint
1 shallot, minced
3 tablespoons olive oil
1 teaspoon Aleppo pepper
Juice from 1 lemon
Salt, to taste
Bread, for serving

Home prep: Combine all ingredients in a jar or other container. Let marinate at least 2 hours before serving. Store in a cooler or refrigerator.

At camp: Serve with slices of crusty bread, bruschetta-style, (as featured in photo, p. 103) or use as a hearty topping in wraps or sandwiches.

Snacks, Sides, and Lunches

GREEK POTATOES (FOIL PACKET)

Adding a bit of chicken broth to these lemony, herby potatoes gives them an extra savory kick.

YIELDS	CAMPING STYLE	EQUIPMENT	DIETARY NOTES
Serves 3–4	Frontcountry 🚗	Metal grill tongs Aluminum foil Hot campfire coals	Gluten-free Dairy-free

4 small Yukon Gold potatoes, quartered
2 tablespoons chicken broth
2–3 sprigs fresh oregano
2–3 sprigs fresh thyme
1 tablespoon olive oil
Salt and pepper, to taste
Juice from 1 lemon

Home prep: Place potatoes in the center of a 2-foot-long foil sheet. Add all ingredients and toss to combine. Wrap tightly, crimping seams of foil to keep any liquids from leaking. Wrap in another sheet of foil, then store in a cooler or refrigerator until ready to cook.

At camp: Prepare a campfire for cooking in foil packets (see p. 109). Cook over hot coals, rotating with tongs occasionally, until potatoes are tender, 25–30 minutes.

Snacks, Sides, and Lunches

HOW TO COOK IN FOIL PACKETS

Use this method for the following recipes:

Greek Potatoes
Tilapia with Vegetables
Dark Chocolate–Blueberry Banana Boats
Orange Chocolate Brownies

Cooking in foil packets allows you to do all the prep at home, so you can relax in camp after mealtime rather than cleaning dishes. It's perfect for a crowd with different tastes or diets since everyone can add or omit ingredients as they like. This method does require a bit of planning, however, since you'll need a fire that has burned down enough to give you hot coals. Be sure to check local fire restrictions and that you can procure enough firewood before committing yourself to any of these recipes.

EQUIPMENT
Metal grill tongs
Aluminum foil
Hot campfire coals

You won't need a giant bonfire to cook your packets, but you will need to give the logs enough time to burn down into hot embers. Simply keep the fire going, adding more wood as needed, until there are bright orange and ashy embers in the middle of the fire. Make sure you have an area within the fire ring (along the edge) that is large enough to accommodate all your foil packets. When a good number of embers are glowing hot, use tongs to move them into the cooking area. Spread them out in an even layer, then add your packets on top, continuing to stoke the fire as needed and move fresh coals around the packets. Rotate the packets occasionally to make sure they're cooking evenly. Cooking time will vary depending on ingredients, but keep some extra foil on hand in case you need to rewrap one of the packets after checking for doneness.

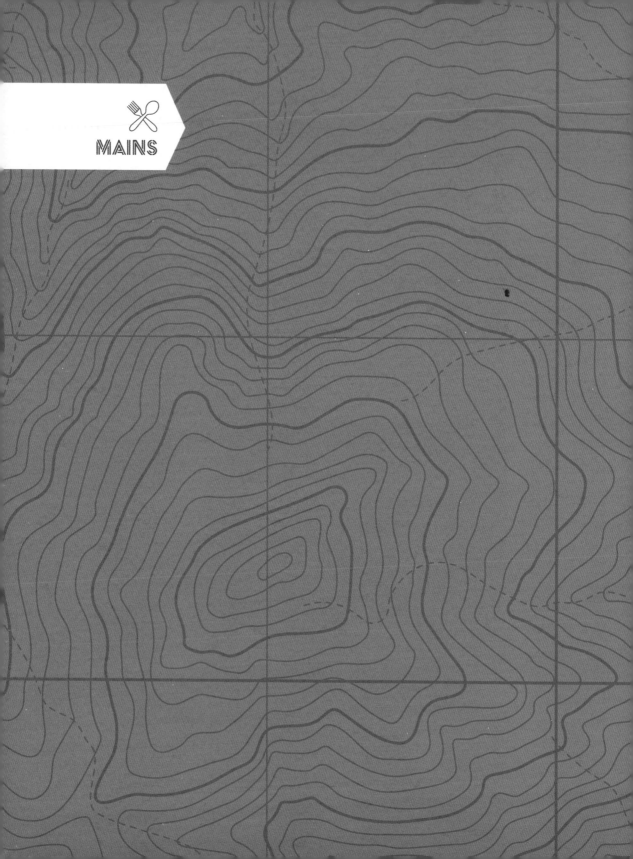

MAINS

MAINS

Note: 🚶 *= backpacking-friendly recipes*

BACKCOUNTRY CHOWDER

With a few pantry staples and fresh ingredients, it's easy to make a chowder base and then add your choice of protein or dehydrated vegetables to finish it. Whichever route you go, it's important to dice the potato into very small chunks so it cooks quickly. Equally important is to add the milk toward the end of cooking and temper it. If you don't, you run the risk of curdling it or having it scorch and stick to the bottom of the pot, leaving you with a very difficult cleaning task (I learned the hard way).

YIELDS	CAMPING STYLE	EQUIPMENT	DIETARY NOTES
Serves 2–3	Backcountry 🚶	Lightweight cook set Backpacking stove Dehydrator	Gluten-free 🌾

1 cup milk powder
¼ cup instant mashed potato flakes
3 cups water, divided
1 medium Yukon Gold potato
2 bouillon cubes
2 tablespoons dried minced onion
1 bay leaf
Salt and pepper, to taste
1 teaspoon smoked paprika
Crackers or bread, for serving

PROTEIN OR VEGETARIAN OPTIONS (CHOOSE ONE, OR MIX AND MATCH)

2 2.5-ounce salmon packets, drained
3 6-ounce cans chopped clams, drained
1 cup dehydrated corn kernels
  (see recipe, p. 44)

Home prep: Combine milk powder and potato flakes in a zip-top bag or other container. Pack other ingredients separately.

At camp: Mix powdered milk and potato flakes into 1 cup water, then set aside.

Dice potato and add to pot with 2 cups water, bouillon cubes, minced onion, and bay leaf (if using corn kernels, add with potatoes). Bring to a boil, then reduce heat and simmer until potatoes are cooked through, about 10 minutes. When potatoes are done, add salmon or clams, if using.

Add ½ cup of the hot liquid to the bowl with milk and potato flake mixture to temper it. Stir to combine, then add to the pot. Remove from heat and let sit a few minutes, stirring frequently, to allow potato flakes to rehydrate. Season with salt, pepper, and paprika, then serve with crackers or bread, if desired.

BLACK BEAN SOUP

This recipe calls for dehydrated black beans and corn, recipes you'll find in the dehydrator section. The sweet potato can be swapped out for yam, regular potato, or another root vegetable, such as carrot or parsnip, if desired. Whichever type you choose, be sure to dice it into small pieces so it cooks quickly.

YIELDS	CAMPING STYLE	EQUIPMENT	DIETARY NOTES
Serves 2–3	Backcountry 🚶	Lightweight cook set Backpacking stove Dehydrator	Vegan Gluten-free Dairy-free

1 cup dehydrated black beans (see recipe, p. 45)
½ cup dehydrated corn (see recipe, p. 44)
1 tablespoon dried minced onion
3 bouillon cubes
1 teaspoon ground cumin
1 teaspoon ground coriander
1 teaspoon garlic powder
½ teaspoon chipotle powder
3 cups water
1 small sweet potato (about ¼ pound), diced into ¼-inch pieces
Optional garnishes: sliced avocado, lime wedges

Home prep: Combine all ingredients, except for sweet potato, water, and garnishes, in a zip-top bag or other container. Pack sweet potato and garnishes separately.

At camp: Add the bag of dry ingredients to a pot with the water and let soak to help rehydrate beans, about 15 minutes. Meanwhile, dice sweet potato and add to the pot. Bring to a boil, then reduce heat, cover, and simmer until beans and corn are rehydrated and the potato is cooked through, 10–15 minutes, stirring occasionally. Serve with avocado slices and lime wedges, if desired.

Mains

Wild Eats: Campsite Cooking

MUSHROOM AND QUINOA SOUP

This soup uses dehydrated mushrooms and vegetables. Dehydrating your own mushrooms is far more cost-effective, but store-bought dried mushrooms will work fine as well. Use red or white quinoa, as other varieties require longer cooking times. Letting the ingredients soak while you set up camp or relax gives them a head start in the rehydrating process, cutting down on the amount of time and fuel needed for cooking.

YIELDS	CAMPING STYLE	EQUIPMENT	DIETARY NOTES
Serves 2–3	Backcountry 🏃	Lightweight cook set Backpacking stove Dehydrator	Vegan Gluten-free Dairy-free 🌱 🌾 🥛

1 ounce dehydrated mushrooms (see recipe, p. 43)
1 ounce dehydrated mixed soup vegetables
    such as corn, peas, carrots (see recipe, p. 44)
1 tablespoon dried minced onion
¼ cup quinoa, red or white variety
3 bouillon cubes
3½ cups water

Home prep: Combine all ingredients except water in a zip-top bag or other container.

At camp: Add all ingredients to a pot with the water and let soak for 20 minutes. Then bring to a boil, reduce heat, cover, and simmer until quinoa is soft and vegetables are cooked and rehydrated, about 15 minutes.

Mains

SOBA NOODLE AND SHIITAKE MUSHROOM SOUP

Dried soba noodles typically come packaged in bundles of three—you'll need only two for this recipe. You can use store-bought dried mushrooms; however, dehydrating your own is far more cost-effective (see p. 43). Get a head start on rehydrating by letting the mushrooms soak while you set up camp or relax.

YIELDS	CAMPING STYLE	EQUIPMENT	DIETARY NOTES
Serves 2–3	Backcountry 🥾	Lightweight cook set Backpacking stove Dehydrator	Vegan Dairy-free V 🗵

1 ounce dehydrated shiitake mushrooms (see recipe, p. 43)
2 bouillon cubes
1 tablespoon ground ginger
1 tablespoon ground coriander
3 tablespoons soy sauce
4 cups water
2 bundles dried soba noodles (about 6 ounces)
1 sheet nori, torn into 1-inch pieces
Optional garnishes: hot sauce, lime wedges

Home prep: Combine dehydrated mushrooms, bouillon cubes, ginger, and coriander in a zip-top bag. Pack other ingredients separately.

At camp: Add mushrooms, bouillon cubes, ginger, coriander, and soy sauce to a pot with the water and soak for 20 minutes. Bring to a boil and cook until mushrooms are soft, about 10 minutes, then add noodles and nori pieces. Reduce heat and gently boil until noodles are cooked, about 5 minutes longer. Serve with hot sauce and lime wedges, if desired.

Mains

MACARONI AND CHEESE

Taking cheese into the backcountry during the sweltering dog days of summer is not the best idea; however, if your destination is more temperate, there are a few hardy cheeses that can survive a day or two without refrigeration. Avoid anything too soft—a hard, well-aged cheese, such as gouda, works well for this recipe. Likewise, butter will keep unrefrigerated; just be sure to keep it well wrapped to avoid a mess. To keep cheese as fresh as possible, don't pre-cut or shred it. If you cut it into small pieces at camp, it should melt into the sauce just fine.

YIELDS	CAMPING STYLE	EQUIPMENT	DIETARY NOTES
Serves 2–3	Backcountry 🚶	Lightweight cook set Backpacking stove	Vegetarian

1 teaspoon ground mustard
1 teaspoon Cajun seasoning
8 ounces dried macaroni
⅓ cup plus 3 tablespoons milk powder
1½ cups water, plus additional for cooking pasta
6 ounces hard, aged cheese, such as gouda
2 tablespoons butter
2 tablespoons all-purpose flour
Salt and pepper, to taste

Home prep: Combine ground mustard and Cajun seasoning in a zip-top bag. Pack other ingredients separately.

At camp: Boil pasta until tender, 6–8 minutes or according to package directions. Drain, then set aside. Reconstitute milk powder with the water then set aside.

Meanwhile, dice cheese into ¼-inch pieces and set aside. In a pot over medium heat, melt butter and add flour to make a roux (see p. 60). Cook until lightly browned, stirring constantly, about 1–2 minutes. Add reconstituted milk, cheese, ground mustard, and Cajun seasoning, and simmer over low heat, continuing to stir, until cheese has melted and sauce has thickened. Add pasta, stir to combine, season with salt and pepper, then serve.

Mains

BACKCOUNTRY BOLOGNESE

This recipe uses dehydrated or freeze-dried ingredients, but sub in fresh ingredients as desired. See recipes for Tomato Leather (p. 42) and Dehydrated Ground Meat (p. 46), which can be prepared well in advance of your trip, or purchase these online or at an outdoor store. Any pasta will do, but I'm partial to egg noodles, which cook quickly. This recipe makes a thick sauce, which can be thinned by reserving some of the water from the cooked pasta.

YIELDS	CAMPING STYLE	EQUIPMENT
Serves 2	Backcountry or frontcountry 🥾🚗	Lightweight cook set Backpacking stove Dehydrator

¾ cup (77 grams) dehydrated ground beef (see recipe, p. 46), or substitute with ¼ pound fresh ground beef

1.5 ounces tomato leather (see recipe, p. 42), or 2 cups prepared tomato sauce and omit water

⅓ cup milk powder

1 bouillon cube

1 teaspoon dried oregano

1 teaspoon red pepper flakes

Pinch ground nutmeg

Salt and pepper, to taste

2 cups water, plus additional for cooking pasta and to thin sauce, if needed

8 ounces dried pasta, such as egg noodles

Optional garnish: shaved parmesan

Home prep: Combine all dehydrated ingredients and spices (except water, pasta, and parmesan) in a zip-top bag or other sealed container. Pack other ingredients separately.

At camp: Boil pasta until tender, 6–8 minutes or according to package directions. Drain, then set aside.

Combine all ingredients except pasta in a pot and add 2 cups of water. Bring to a boil, cover, and simmer over low heat, stirring occasionally, until tomato leather is blended and meat is rehydrated, 10–15 minutes. If the sauce becomes too thick, add water a few tablespoons at a time. Toss sauce with cooked pasta and serve. Add parmesan if desired.

MUSHROOM PASTA

This recipe calls for dehydrated tomato sauce and dehydrated mushrooms, which can be prepared days (or even weeks) in advance of your trip. Any type of pasta will do, but shorter varieties tend to cook faster. This recipe makes a fairly thick sauce, which can be thinned out by reserving some of the water from the cooked pasta. If your trip isn't in a climate that's too hot, a small block of parmesan cheese will keep, but to keep it fresh, slice it into thin shavings at camp rather than ahead of time.

YIELDS	CAMPING STYLE	EQUIPMENT	DIETARY NOTES
Serves 2	Backcountry or frontcountry 🥾🚗	Lightweight cook set Backpacking stove Dehydrator	Vegan and dairy-free (without parmesan) 🌱⊘

1.5 ounces tomato leather (see recipe, p. 42), or sub in 2 cups prepared
    tomato sauce and omit water)
1 ounce dehydrated mushrooms (see recipe, p. 43)
1 bouillon cube
½ tablespoon dried oregano
½ tablespoon dried basil
1 teaspoon garlic powder
Salt and pepper, to taste
2 cups water, plus additional for cooking pasta and to thin sauce, if needed
8 ounces dried pasta
Optional garnish: shaved parmesan

Home prep: Combine all ingredients (except water, pasta, and parmesan) in a zip-top bag or other sealed container. Pack other ingredients separately.

At camp: Boil pasta until tender, 6–8 minutes or according to package directions. Drain, then set aside.

    Combine all ingredients in a pot except pasta and add 2 cups water. Let soak 15–20 minutes, then bring to a boil, cover, and simmer over low heat, stirring occasionally, until tomato leather is blended and mushrooms are rehydrated, another 10–15 minutes. If sauce becomes too thick, add water a few tablespoons at a time (use reserved water from cooked pasta, if desired). Toss sauce with cooked noodles and serve. Add parmesan if desired.

Mains

RED LENTIL CURRY

For a quick, hearty backcountry meal, red lentils pack a lot of bang for their buck. Look for a faster-cooking variety (Bob's Red Mill is my go-to) that doesn't need soaking. Coconut milk powder can be found in most well-stocked grocery stores or online.

YIELDS	CAMPING STYLE	EQUIPMENT	DIETARY NOTES
Serves 2	Backcountry 🏃	Lightweight cook set Backpacking stove	Vegan Gluten-free Dairy-free

¾ cup red lentils
2 bouillon cubes
1 tablespoon curry powder
1 teaspoon ground ginger powder
1 teaspoon turmeric
1 tablespoon coconut oil
1 small sweet potato, diced into ¼-inch pieces
¼ cup coconut milk powder
2 cups water, plus additional to thin stew, if needed
Salt, to taste
Optional garnishes: cilantro, lime wedges, sriracha

Home prep: Combine all ingredients except coconut oil, sweet potato, coconut milk powder, water, and garnishes in a zip-top bag. Pack other ingredients separately.

At camp: Heat oil over medium heat. Add the bag of dry ingredients and lightly stir-fry until spices are fragrant, about 1 minute. Add the sweet potato, coconut milk powder, and 2 cups of water. Bring to a boil, cover, and simmer over low heat, stirring occasionally, until sweet potatoes are cooked through and lentils begin to break down, 10–15 minutes. If the stew becomes too thick, add water a few tablespoons at a time. Salt to taste, and serve with desired garnishes on the side.

Mains

ANCHO RED CHILI

It's definitely worth seeking out ancho chile powder for its sweet, smoky flavor, but other varieties will do in a pinch. As this recipe calls for coffee, consider brewing an extra cup in the morning to save for later, or you can substitute another liquid such as beer, stock, or water. This chili can be cooked as easily on a grill grate over a fire in a cast-iron pan or Dutch oven as it can be with a skillet on a two-burner camp stove.

YIELDS	CAMPING STYLE	EQUIPMENT	DIETARY NOTES
Serves 4	Frontcountry 🚗	Cast-iron skillet or Dutch oven Two-burner stove or hot campfire coals	Gluten-free Dairy-free (with vegan chocolate)

1 white onion, diced
1 jalapeño, de-seeded and diced
2½ tablespoons ancho chile powder
1 teaspoon ground coriander
1 tablespoon ground cumin
1 teaspoon garlic powder
1 tablespoon vegetable oil
1 pound ground beef or bison
Salt and pepper, to taste
1 14-ounce can diced, fire-roasted
   tomatoes

1 bouillon cube
1 cup black coffee
1 15-ounce can beans, such as red,
   black, or pinto
1½ ounces Mexican (or dark) chocolate
Optional garnishes: sour cream,
   avocado, cilantro, lime wedges,
   shredded cheese, hot sauce,
   pickled jalapeños, diced onion

Home prep: Combine diced onion and jalapeño in one container. Combine chile powder, coriander, cumin, and garlic powder in another container. Pack other ingredients separately.

At camp: Heat oil over medium-high heat. Add meat to the pan, season lightly with salt and pepper and cook until well-browned and liquid has evaporated, 5–10 minutes. Add onion and jalapeño and cook until lightly browned, about 5 minutes. Add chile powder, coriander, cumin, and garlic powder and continue to cook until spices are fragrant, about 1 minute. Add tomatoes, bouillon, coffee, and beans. Bring to a boil, reduce heat to low, and stir in chocolate. Simmer, partially covered, until stew has thickened, 15–20 minutes. Serve with desired garnishes on the side.

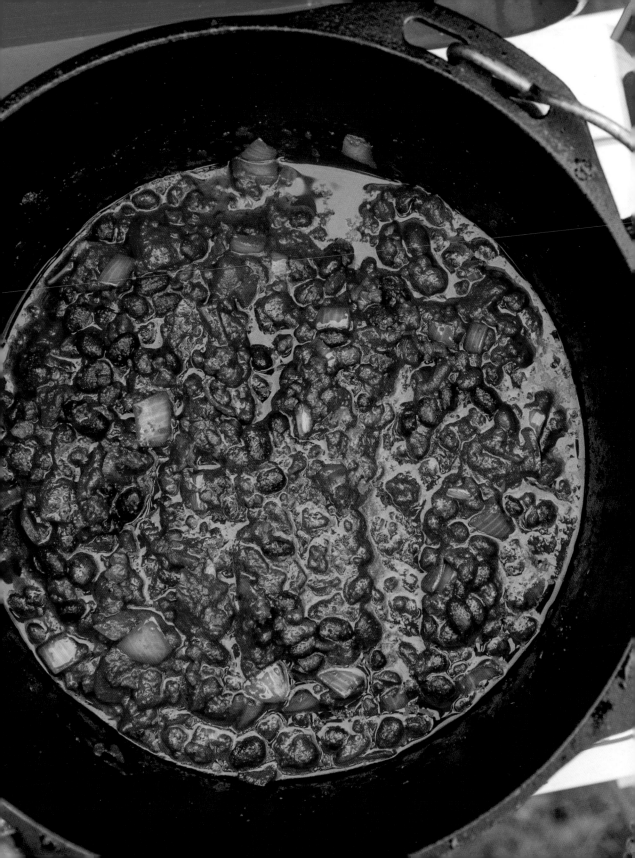

HOW TO KNOW YOUR CHILE POWDERS

When you're cooking with chile powder, it's important to know what type you're using. Avoid generic chile powders, unless the type of chile is listed in the ingredients. Heat level and flavor differ drastically among them, so avoid scorching your taste buds by choosing carefully. And don't confuse *chile* powder with *chili* powder, the latter of which does contain chiles, but also other spices commonly used for chili, the dish. In this book, I'm always referring to *chile* powder, which is usually made from just one type of chile.

Aleppo: This Middle Eastern variety is the dried form of a Halaby pepper. It's mild, sweet, and flavorful. Try this with Marinated White Beans (p. 104) or Shakshuka (p. 76).

Ancho: Made from ripened, dried poblano pepper, ancho is renowned for its fruity, earthy flavor, mild heat level, and hints of smoke. It makes a good backbone for spice mixtures where you don't want an overwhelming level of heat. This is what I primarily use in chilis (see Ancho Red Chili, p. 130).

Cayenne: Like chipotles, cayennes are best used alongside milder types if you want to give your finished dish some extra kick. They lack the earthy, fruity depth of ancho or New Mexico red chiles, but are far hotter. If the chili recipes in this book aren't hot enough for you, add some cayenne to kick it up a notch.

Chipotle: Made from ripened, smoked jalapeños, this one packs a surprising level of heat. If used on its own, chipotle chile powder can be very hot and overwhelmingly smoky, but it makes a great sidekick to a more versatile type of chile, such as ancho or New Mexico. Chipotles are also commonly found canned or jarred whole, packed in a spicy tomato sauce, known as *chipotles en adobo*. Add chipotle to any chili or other dish where you want a smoky flavor.

Guajillo: This dried form of a morita pepper is well worth adding to your chile powder collection if you can find it. Sweet and slightly tangy, the spice's heat level is similar to a New Mexico red chile.

New Mexico red: Like anchos, New Mexico red chiles are versatile and have manageable levels of heat. They have a sweet, earthy flavor and are usually medium-hot. This would be a good base chile powder for any type of chili.

Paprika: This sweet Eastern European spice comes from ripe red peppers. Smoked varieties are also commonly found and will be labeled mild or hot. This one is integral to the flavor in Shakshuka (p. 76).

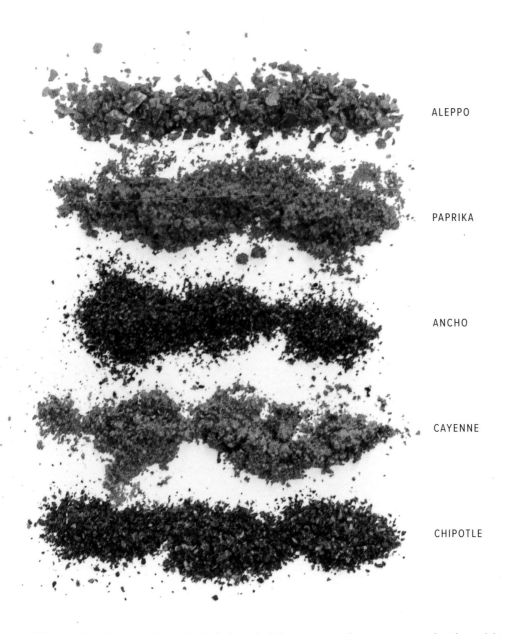

ALEPPO

PAPRIKA

ANCHO

CAYENNE

CHIPOTLE

Where to buy: You should be able to find most of these at a regular grocery store, but they might not be in the spice aisle. The bulk section of many grocery stores stocks some of the less common varieties, while the international section often has a decent selection of Mexican and New Mexican chile varieties in particular. A local store that stocks Latin American or Middle Eastern foods is also a great option.

BLACK BEAN AND SWEET POTATO CHILI

This hearty, spicy vegetarian chili is as tasty as it is adaptable. Make it vegan by using vegan chocolate, or adjust the heat by using more or less chile powder or a milder type. This can be cooked as easily on a grill grate over a fire in a cast-iron pan or Dutch oven as it can be with a skillet on a two-burner camp stove.

YIELDS	CAMPING STYLE	EQUIPMENT	DIETARY NOTES
Serves 4	Frontcountry 🚗	Cast-iron skillet or Dutch oven Two-burner stove or hot campfire coals	Vegan and dairy-free (with vegan chocolate) Gluten-free V 🌿 ⊘

1 medium sweet potato
  (about ½ pound), diced
1 red onion, diced
1 jalapeño, de-seeded and diced
2 tablespoons ancho chile powder
1 tablespoon Mexican oregano
  (or Mediterranean in a pinch)
1 teaspoon ground coriander
1 teaspoon ground cumin
1 teaspoon garlic powder

1 tablespoon vegetable oil
1 14-ounce can diced tomatoes
2 15-ounce cans black beans
1 ounce dark chocolate
1 bouillon cube
1 cup water
Optional garnishes: avocado, cilantro,
  lime wedges, shredded cheese,
  diced onion

Home prep: Combine sweet potato, onion, and jalapeño in one container. In a separate container, combine chile powder, oregano, coriander, cumin, and garlic powder. Pack other ingredients separately.

At camp: Heat oil over medium heat. Add sweet potato, onion, and jalapeño. Sauté until lightly browned, about 5 minutes. Add spices and continue to cook for 1 minute. Add tomatoes, beans, chocolate, bouillon cube, and 1 cup water. Bring to a boil and then simmer, partially covered, until potatoes are cooked through, about 15 minutes. Serve with desired garnishes on the side.

DUTCH OVEN MUSHROOM AND ROOT VEGETABLE STEW

All the warming comfort of old-fashioned beef stew—without the meat. Mixed mushrooms with big chunks of root vegetables are simmered in a thick gravy, resulting in a dish that sticks to your ribs without putting you in a food coma. Use any root vegetables you'd like, but I prefer a mix of parsnips, carrots, and potatoes. For mushrooms, mix and match as desired, using varieties such as portobello, cremini, shiitake, oyster, or other wild types. Serve this stew as is or atop egg noodles, mashed potatoes, or polenta.

YIELDS	CAMPING STYLE	EQUIPMENT	DIETARY NOTES
Serves 4–6	Frontcountry 🚗	Dutch oven Charcoal chimney starter (or hot campfire coals)	Vegetarian Dairy-free ⊘ 🍶

1½ pounds mixed mushrooms,
   cut into 1-inch pieces
1½ pounds mixed root vegetables,
   cut into 1-inch pieces
½ pound cipollini or pearl onions,
   peeled but left whole
6 cloves garlic, peeled and
   roughly chopped
2 tablespoons olive oil
¼ cup tomato paste
1 cup red wine

1 tablespoon Worcestershire sauce
1 tablespoon tamari sauce
3 bouillon cubes
2 bay leaves
3 cups plus 3 tablespoons water
3 tablespoons cornstarch
Mashed potatoes, polenta,
   or egg noodles, for serving
Optional garnish: chopped parsley
Salt and pepper, to taste

Home prep: Mix all cut vegetables together in a zip-top bag or other container. Pack other ingredients separately.

At camp: Prepare Dutch oven for roasting, starting with an even layer of coals underneath the pot. Heat oil until shimmering, then add vegetables. Cook uncovered until mushrooms have released their liquid and it has evaporated, about 15 minutes.

Meanwhile, preheat the lid by adding a layer of coals on top of it.

Add tomato paste to the pot, stir to combine, and cook, uncovered, until paste has darkened slightly, about 2 minutes. Add red wine, scraping any browned bits from the bottom. Let come to a boil, then add Worcestershire sauce, tamari, bouillon cubes,

Mains

bay leaves, and 3 cups of water. Cover with the preheated lid and cook until root vegetables are done, about 20 minutes, moving coals around as necessary to keep the stew at a simmer.

Before serving, mix cornstarch with 3 tablespoons of water, then add to stew (make sure stew is at least bubbling). Stir and cook uncovered until thickened, 3–5 minutes. Serve as is, or over mashed potatoes, polenta, or egg noodles, topped with chopped parsley. Add salt and pepper, as desired.

DUTCH OVEN CHICKEN CACCIATORE

Cacciatore translates to "hunter-style," and there are as many variations of this Italian classic as there are chefs, so don't be afraid to stray from the main recipe. Serve as is or atop pasta or a grain of your choice (such as orzo or pearled couscous).

YIELDS	CAMPING STYLE	EQUIPMENT	DIETARY NOTES
Serves 4–6	Frontcountry 🚗	Dutch oven Charcoal chimney starter (or hot campfire coals)	Dairy-free 🥛

½ pound cremini mushrooms, quartered
1 onion, thinly sliced
1 red bell pepper, thinly sliced
5 garlic cloves, roughly chopped
2 pounds chicken thighs and/or
    drumsticks, bone in, skin on
¼ cup flour

¼ cup olive oil
1 cup white wine (or chicken broth)
1 28-ounce can crushed tomatoes
1 bay leaf
1 cup Kalamata or mixed olives
Salt and pepper, to taste
Optional garnish: fresh parsley

Home prep: Mix all cut vegetables together in a zip-top bag or other container. In a separate container, combine chicken with flour, season with salt and pepper, and mix well to dredge chicken. Pack other ingredients separately.

At camp: Prepare Dutch oven for roasting, starting with an even layer of coals underneath the pot. Heat oil until shimmering, then add chicken. Cook uncovered until chicken is browned on all sides, about 10 minutes. Meanwhile, preheat the lid by adding a layer of coals on top of it. When chicken is browned, remove from the pot and set aside.

Add mushrooms, onion, bell pepper, and garlic to the pot. Cook until mushrooms have released their liquid and it has evaporated, about 10 minutes. Add wine (or broth), scraping up any browned bits on the bottom of the pan, and let simmer until it has evaporated slightly, about 5 minutes.

Add tomatoes, bay leaf, olives, and chicken to the pot and mix well to combine. Cover with preheated lid and cook until stew has thickened and chicken is falling off the bone, about 30 minutes, moving coals around as necessary to keep stew at a simmer. Add salt and pepper as desired and top with parsley.

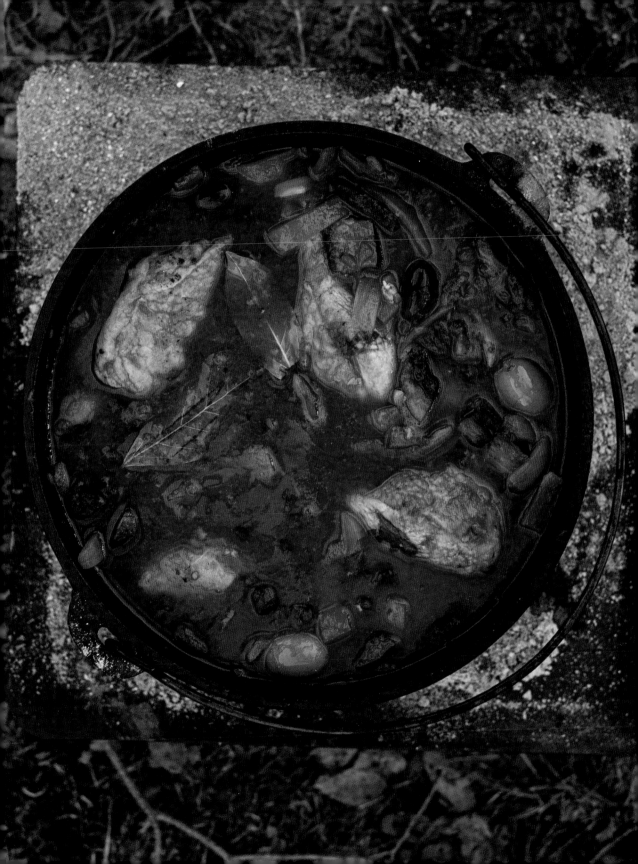

DUTCH OVEN CHICKEN AND BLACK BEAN ENCHILADAS

Pull meat from a store-bought rotisserie chicken or pre-cook chicken breasts or thighs. A whole rotisserie chicken will yield a bit more meat, which you can save for another use (chicken salad sandwiches, etc.). A 10-inch Dutch oven holds about 8 enchiladas using 6-inch flour tortillas. Use whichever type of enchilada sauce you prefer—red, green, or both for "Christmas" style.

YIELDS	CAMPING STYLE	EQUIPMENT	DIETARY NOTES
Serves 4–6	Frontcountry 🚗	Dutch oven Charcoal chimney starter (or hot campfire coals)	Gluten-free (with corn tortillas instead of flour)

2 cups cooked chicken, chopped
1 14.5-ounce can black beans, drained
3 cups shredded Monterey Jack cheese, divided
2½ cups enchilada sauce, red, green, or both
8 6-inch flour tortillas
Salt and pepper, to taste
Optional garnishes: sliced avocado, lime wedges, chopped cilantro,
    sour cream, pickled jalapeños, hot sauce

Home prep: Combine chicken, black beans, and 1 cup shredded cheese in a zip-top bag or other leak-proof container. Pack other ingredients separately.

At camp: Prepare ¾ of a chimney full of charcoal. When coals are lit, arrange them on the lid of the Dutch oven, using enough to mostly cover it, about 15–20 coals, reserving 7–10 coals for putting underneath the oven.

Pour a layer of enchilada sauce in the bottom of the Dutch oven. Roll chicken, bean, and cheese mixture into tortillas and place in the pot seam side down, repeating until 8 enchiladas are snugly packed in. Pour remaining sauce evenly over enchiladas, then top with remaining cheese (do this before putting it on coals to avoid burning yourself).

Place Dutch oven over coals and cover with the preheated lid. Bake until sauce has thickened and cheese is browned and bubbly, 25–30 minutes. Cool 5–10 minutes before serving with salt and pepper and garnishes, as desired.

Mains

CHANA MASALA

This warming chickpea and tomato stew, a popular Indian dish, gets a hand from Thai red curry paste, which saves you the task of chopping and mashing ginger and garlic. Serve as is or over rice, with plenty of warm naan or flour tortillas to mop up the medium-spicy sauce.

YIELDS	CAMPING STYLE	EQUIPMENT	DIETARY NOTES
Serves 3–4	Frontcountry 🚗	Cast-iron skillet or medium pot Two-burner stove or hot campfire coals	Vegan Gluten-free (with corn tortillas instead of flour) Dairy-free V 🌾 🥛

1 tablespoon garam masala
1 tablespoon ground cumin
½ tablespoon ground coriander
½ tablespoon garlic powder
1 onion, diced
1 jalapeño, de-seeded and diced
1 tablespoon brown mustard seeds
2 tablespoons coconut oil

1 tablespoon red curry paste
2 14-ounce cans chickpeas, drained
1 28-ounce can crushed tomatoes
Salt and pepper, to taste
Optional garnishes: chopped cilantro, lime wedges, hot sauce, yogurt
Naan or tortillas, for serving

Home prep: Combine garam masala, cumin, coriander, and garlic powder in a leak-proof container. Combine onion, jalapeño, and mustard seeds in a plastic bag or other container. Pack other ingredients separately.

At camp: Heat oil over medium-high heat. Add onion, jalapeño, and mustard seeds. Cook until mustard seeds stop sputtering and onion has softened, 5–10 minutes. Add spice mixture and curry paste, stirring frequently to keep from sticking to the bottom, until fragrant, 1–2 minutes. Add chickpeas and tomatoes, bring to a boil, then reduce heat and simmer until stew has thickened, 10–15 minutes. Season with salt and pepper. Serve with desired garnishes on the side.

Mains

GREEN CHILE STEW

Roasted green chiles can sometimes be found frozen or refrigerated in grocery stores during late summer and early fall, which is the harvest season. If not, roast, peel, and dice them before tossing them in a cooler (see p. 147), or if you have time, roast them over a camp stove burner (or open fire for extra smoky flavor). They run the gamut from mild to scorching and are not always labeled, so beware of what you're buying. If in doubt, substitute some or all of the Hatch or Anaheim chiles with poblanos, which are milder, or omit the jalapeño.

YIELDS	CAMPING STYLE	EQUIPMENT	DIETARY NOTES
Serves 4	Frontcountry 🚗	Cast-iron skillet or Dutch oven Two-burner stove or hot campfire coals	Gluten-free Dairy-free

1 white onion, diced
1 jalapeño, de-seeded and diced
1 teaspoon ground coriander
1 teaspoon ground cumin
1 teaspoon garlic powder
1 tablespoon vegetable oil
1 pound ground pork, beef, or bison
Salt and pepper, to taste
1 Yukon Gold potato, diced into ¼-inch pieces

1½ cups roasted, peeled, and diced green chiles
1 15-ounce can hominy, drained
1 16-ounce jar tomatillo salsa
1 bouillon cube
1 cup water
Optional garnishes: sour cream, avocado, cilantro, lime wedges, shredded cheese, pickled jalapeños, diced onion

Home prep: Combine diced onion and jalapeño in one container. In a separate container, combine coriander, cumin, and garlic powder. Pack other ingredients separately.

At camp: Heat oil over medium-high heat. Add meat to the pan, season lightly with salt and pepper and cook until well-browned and liquid has evaporated, 5–10 minutes. Add potato, onion, and jalapeño and cook until lightly browned, about 5 minutes. Add coriander, cumin, and garlic powder and continue to cook for 1 minute. Add diced green chiles, hominy, salsa, bouillon cube, and 1 cup of water. Bring to a boil and then simmer, partially covered, until potatoes are cooked through and stew has thickened, 15–20 minutes. Serve with desired garnishes on the side.

HOW TO SELECT AND PREPARE FRESH GREEN CHILES

If you can't locate a good source for freshly roasted green chiles, it's easy to roast them yourself, at home or at camp. It may seem intimidating at first, but the good news is that it's hard to overdo it when it comes to charring the outside. You're aiming for a very blackened, well-charred skin, which will peel off easily when the chiles are cool enough to handle. Here are a few more tips to help you select and roast your green chiles to perfection:

- **Selecting.** Look for chiles that are smooth and firm, paying special attention to the ends, which tend to deteriorate first.
- **Heat level.** Poblano, sometimes called *pasilla*, chiles are milder than New Mexico or Anaheim chiles. Using a mix of both adds complexity to the final dish, but if you don't want to risk making it too spicy, go with poblanos.

CHARRING METHODS

- **Under a broiler.** Heat broiler on high. Place chiles on a rimmed, foil-lined baking sheet and roast until blackened all over, turning occasionally. It's a good idea to open a window or turn on a kitchen fan while doing this.
- **With a propane burner or camp stove.** Turn on the burner to medium-high and place chiles directly on the burner over the flame. Watch closely, using tongs to turn them frequently until well charred on all sides.
- **Next steps.** When chiles are blackened on all sides, wrap tightly in aluminum foil. Let sit until cool enough to handle, 15–20 minutes. When cool, trim stems and slice

in half lengthwise, laying the chile flat with the inside facing up. Scrape the seeds and ribs from the inside with a knife. Flip over and, using the same method, scrape off the charred skin (it's okay to have a few patches of skin left on). Your chile is now roasted, peeled, de-seeded, and ready to use.

Note: I highly recommend wearing rubber gloves while handling the chiles. Even if your hands aren't particularly sensitive to capsaicin (the compound that gives chiles their heat), you're bound to touch your face or rub your eyes at some point during the process.

CORNMEAL-CRUSTED TROUT WITH DILL-CAPER SAUCE

Whether you catch the trout yourself or take the easy route, you'll want to work with whole, skin-on, butterflied trout fillets (or individual fillets for larger trout). If you're hoping to catch your dinner in the backcountry, you don't need to pack much more than a few lemons for serving. If bringing a cooler is an option, consider pairing the trout with a tasty yogurt-based dill and caper sauce (recipe follows, p. 150).

YIELDS	CAMPING STYLE	EQUIPMENT	DIETARY NOTES
Serves 2–4	Frontcountry or backcountry 🚗 🥾	Cast-iron or lightweight backpacking skillet Two-burner or backpacking stove	Dairy-free (without Dill-Caper Sauce)

¼ cup cornmeal

¼ cup flour

2 whole trout, butterflied, bones removed (about 8–10 inches each)

Salt and pepper, to taste

2 tablespoons fresh dill, chopped

¼ cup vegetable oil

1–2 sliced lemons, as a garnish

Home prep: Combine cornmeal and flour in a zip-top bag. Pack other ingredients separately.

At camp: Season fillets with salt and pepper on both sides, then sprinkle with chopped dill. Dredge fillets in cornmeal and flour mixture until well coated.

Heat oil in a skillet over medium-high heat. Working with one fish at a time, fry skin-side down until crisped, 2–3 minutes. Flip and cook the other side until browned and fish is cooked through, another 2–3 minutes. Remove from heat, repeat with remaining fish, finishing with a squeeze of lemon juice before serving, if desired.

Mains

Dill-Caper Sauce

Serve with Cornmeal-Crusted Trout (p. 148).

YIELDS	DIETARY NOTES
Makes about 1 cup	Vegetarian
	∅

½ cup Greek yogurt
2 tablespoons capers
2 tablespoons fresh dill, chopped
1 tablespoon minced shallot
1 teaspoon Dijon mustard
Juice from 1 lemon
½ teaspoon salt

Home prep: Mix ingredients together and store in the refrigerator or cooler. Sauce can be prepared up to a week in advance.

FLANK STEAK FAJITAS

Prepare the marinade and chop the veggies ahead of time for a meal that comes together quickly in camp. Swap the steak for chicken breasts if you want a different protein, following the same procedure. If you can't find flank steak, skirt steak is another great option for fajitas. Add your choice of garnishes, preparing them at home or before you start cooking so that they're ready while the fajitas are still sizzling hot.

YIELDS	CAMPING STYLE	EQUIPMENT	DIETARY NOTES
Serves 4–6	Frontcountry	Cast-iron skillet	Dairy-free
		Two-burner stove	

2 pounds flank steak

MARINADE
4 cloves garlic, chopped
Juice from 2 limes
2 chipotle chiles in adobo,
   de-seeded and chopped
¼ cup olive oil
1 tablespoon soy sauce
1 tablespoon Worcestershire sauce
1 tablespoon ground cumin
1 teaspoon pepper

FAJITAS
1 onion, sliced lengthwise
1 poblano pepper, sliced
1 red bell pepper, sliced
Flour (or corn) tortillas
Cooking oil
Optional garnishes: sour cream,
   salsa, guacamole, pickled jalapeños,
   cilantro, lime wedges

Home prep: Combine marinade ingredients, including steak, in a zip-top bag. Marinate for a few hours or overnight in a cooler or refrigerator. Pack onions and peppers together in a separate container. Pack other ingredients separately.

At camp: Heat skillet over medium-high heat. One at a time, heat tortillas until lightly charred and puffy, about 10–20 seconds per side. Wrap warmed tortillas in foil and set aside.

    Remove meat from the marinade and pat dry with a paper towel. Add 1 teaspoon cooking oil to the skillet, heating over medium-high until very hot. Add steak and sear until well-browned, 3–5 minutes per side for medium-rare, or until a meat thermometer registers an internal temperature of 130°F at the thickest part of steak (see

p. 155). Remove from skillet and set aside on a cutting board tented with foil. Let rest 10 minutes before slicing.

Add another teaspoon of oil to the skillet, heating over medium-high heat. Add onions and peppers, cooking until lightly charred. Remove from heat and wrap in foil until ready to serve.

Cut steak into thin slices, cutting against the grain for more tender pieces. Serve with vegetables, warm tortillas, and desired garnishes.

HOW TO COOK A GREAT STEAK

Cooking a steak over an open fire can be intimidating. But follow a few simple guidelines and even novice chefs can turn out perfectly seared steaks cooked to order.

- **Know your cuts.** Ribeye, filet mignon, and New York strip are often the choice cuts for grilling, but others pack as much flavor for a fraction of the price.
- **Let the steak come to room temperature before cooking.** This helps it cook more evenly.
- **Sear in a hot pan.** A cast-iron skillet that is ripping hot, whether you're camping in a national park or in a professional kitchen, is the best tool for the job. Nonstick coatings don't stand up well to the level of heat needed for a good sear. Searing, though, contrary to popular belief, does not "seal in the juices." What it does do is brown the outside, caramelizing the natural sugars in the meat in a process that is known as the w reaction.
- **Use a meat thermometer.** There are all kinds of tricks that backyard chefs try to use, but there's only one foolproof method to ensure you're cooking to the right temperature: using a thermometer, inserted into the thickest part of the meat. For best results, take your steak off the heat when it's a few degrees shy of the target temperature, since it will continue to rise while it rests. The USDA recommends cooking beef steaks to a minimum of 145°F and ground beef to a minimum of 160°F. For steak, the target temperatures are as follows:

  > rare: 125–130°F
  > medium-rare: 130–135°F
  > medium: 135–145°F
  > well: 145–155°F
  > well-done: 155°F and above

- **Let it rest.** If you take a steak off the heat and cut into it right away, the juices will run out of it and the meat will dry out. By letting it rest, you allow the juices to redistribute and settle back into the steak.

Mains

PINEAPPLE TERIYAKI KEBABS

Store-bought teriyaki sauce will work in a pinch, but making your own is easy and means you can adjust the sweetness to your own taste and bring out more complex flavors. You can use the same method for building your cooking fire as detailed in the foil packet instructions (see p. 109); however, note that this recipe calls for a portable grill grate instead. Sirloin tips are a good option for a tender beef cut, but chicken works well too, or double up on the veggies for a vegan meal.

YIELDS	CAMPING STYLE	EQUIPMENT	DIETARY NOTES
Serves 4–6	Frontcountry 🚗	Metal grill tongs Grill grate Hot campfire coals Skewers	Gluten-free (with tamari instead of soy sauce) Dairy-free

FOR TERIYAKI SAUCE MARINADE

1 cup soy sauce (or tamari)

1 cup sake

1 cup mirin (rice wine)

¼ cup brown sugar

Combine all marinade ingredients in a saucepan and bring to a boil over medium heat. Continue to cook until sauce has reduced by about ⅔ (you'll end up with about a cup of sauce). Let cool before using.

FOR KEBABS

1 pound beef sirloin tips, cut into 1½-inch cubes

8 ounces cremini mushrooms, stems removed

2 cups pineapple, cut into 1½-inch cubes

1 red onion, cut into 1½-inch pieces

1 bell pepper, cut into 1½-inch pieces

Home prep: Cut and combine all kebab ingredients in a zip-top bag or other leak-proof container with marinade. Let marinate for at least a few hours or overnight.

At camp: Prepare a campfire for cooking. You won't need a giant bonfire to cook over, but you do need to give the logs enough time to burn down into hot embers. The goal is to keep the fire going, adding more wood as needed, until there are bright orange and ashy embers in the middle of it. Ensure you have an area within the fire ring (along the edge) that is large enough to accommodate a grill grate.

When a good number of embers are glowing hot, use tongs to move them into the cooking area. Spread them out in an even layer, then prop the grill grate on a few rocks so that it's about 6 inches above the coals. Continue to stoke the fire and move fresh coals underneath the grate as needed.

Meanwhile, thread meat and veggies onto skewers (if using wooden skewers, soak in water for at least 30 minutes). Grill until meat is cooked to medium-rare or medium and vegetables are lightly charred, 3–5 minutes per side. Let rest 5 minutes before serving.

Mains

TILAPIA WITH VEGETABLES (FOIL PACKET)

Individually wrapped servings make this recipe easily scalable and customizable. Feel free to experiment with different fish or vegetables.

YIELDS	CAMPING STYLE	EQUIPMENT	DIETARY NOTES
Serves 4	Frontcountry 🚗	Metal grill tongs Aluminum foil Hot campfire coals	Gluten-free Dairy-free

1 bunch asparagus, ends trimmed
1 zucchini, cut into ½-inch-thick slices
Extra-virgin olive oil, for drizzling
Balsamic vinegar, for drizzling
Salt and pepper, to taste
4 6-ounce tilapia fillets
1 lemon, sliced into ¼-inch slices
Fresh thyme sprigs
1 pint cherry tomatoes

Home prep: Place 4 sheets of aluminum foil, each about two feet long, on a work surface. Divide asparagus and zucchini evenly among foil sheets. Drizzle a tablespoon or two each of olive oil and balsamic vinegar, season generously with salt and pepper, then toss to evenly coat vegetables in oil and vinegar. Place a tilapia fillet on top of vegetables, drizzle another bit of oil over fish, then season fish with salt and pepper. Place a few slices of lemon and sprigs of thyme on top of each fillet, then divide cherry tomatoes evenly among the packets. Wrap tightly, crimping seams of foil to keep liquids from leaking. Wrap each packet in another sheet of foil, then store in a cooler or refrigerator until ready to cook.

At camp: Prepare a campfire for cooking in foil packets (see p. 109). Cook packets over hot coals, occasionally rotating with tongs, until vegetables are tender and fish is cooked through, about 20 minutes.

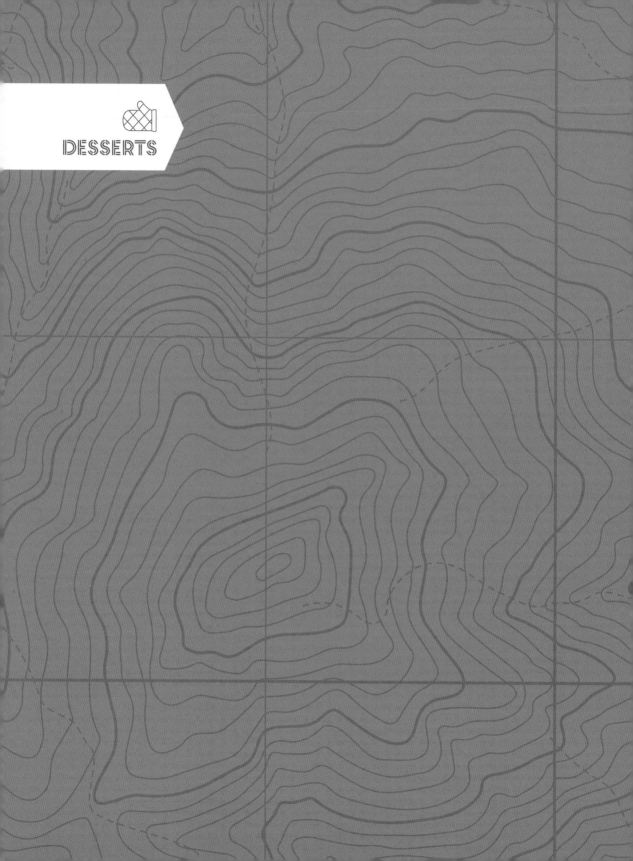

DESSERTS

DESSERTS

Note: 🥾 *= backpacking-friendly recipes*

MEXICAN HOT CHOCOLATE

This recipe is only slightly more involved than adding a packet of cocoa to hot water, but the frothy, creamy, and slightly spicy result is worth your extra effort. Not just any chocolate will do for this—look in the international food aisle or at a Mexican grocery store to find the type of Mexican chocolate you need. Mexican chocolate is made up of ground cacao mixed with granulated sugar and usually contains spices such as cinnamon, allspice, nutmeg, or chiles. Ibarra and Abuelita are two common brands, but there are smaller, artisanal brands to be found in many grocery stores. If you have access to a cooler, you can use 4 cups of milk instead of milk powder. If you're in the backcountry using milk powder, keep it from scorching the bottom of the pot or curdling by tempering it before adding it to the hot chocolate mixture.

YIELDS	CAMPING STYLE	WEQUIPMENT	DIETARY NOTES
Serves 4	Backcountry	Lightweight cook set	Vegetarian
	🚶	Backpacking stove	Gluten-free
			⌀ 🌾

3½–4 ounces Mexican chocolate
4 cups water, divided
2⅓ cups milk powder (or 4 cups milk)
Pinch ground cinnamon
Pinch chile powder
Cinnamon sticks, for serving

Home prep: Pack all ingredients separately.

At camp: Add chocolate to a pot with 2 cups of water and simmer over medium heat, stirring frequently to dissolve chocolate. Meanwhile, mix 2 cups of water with milk powder in a separate container. When chocolate has melted and become frothy, add some of the hot liquid to the milk to temper it and stir. Remove hot chocolate mixture from heat, add in tempered milk, and stir to combine. Serve with a pinch of cinnamon and chile powder in each mug with a cinnamon stick for stirring.

HOW TO MAKE THE PERFECT S'MORES

You don't need a cookbook to tell you how to make s'mores. Of course there are variations, such as using a peanut butter cup instead of chocolate or placing your chocolate-topped graham cracker on a rock next to the fire to slightly melt it first. But let's be honest—the real challenge is the marshmallow. We're all guilty of shoving a marshmallow directly into the flame, setting it on fire, then trying to blow it out (or even more egregious, waving it around and flinging a flaming projectile toward fellow campers). Or, if you didn't wave it around and send it flying or watch it drip off your stick and back into the fire, you likely scraped the crispy, blackened marshmallow onto a graham cracker and just called it good. Because even a bad s'more is still good. But I'm here to tell you, there's a better way. For the perfect marshmallow, there are two forces at work that you need to understand: first, what type of heat works best, and second, how that heat affects the sugar molecules that you're trying to keep from burning to a crisp.

Much like grilling with charcoal, glowing embers (not flames) are ideal for roasting marshmallows. Flames are hotter and more volatile than embers, which emit a gentler, more predictable heat that allows you to monitor your mallow's progress without instantly turning it to ash. This means letting the fire burn down a bit and roasting your marshmallow closer to the embers at the base of the fire rather than directly in the flame.

As for attaining that perfect golden-brown color, the process is called caramelization. Sugar itself is a single type of molecule, but when heat is applied to it, it breaks down into different molecules and creates hundreds of complex new flavor compounds, ranging from nutty and aromatic to bitter and astringent. The more heat that is applied, the less those precious sugar molecules remain and instead are replaced by more bitter compounds, which is why a pitch-black marshmallow is probably better off melting into the fire. The sweet spot, literally and figuratively, is somewhere in the middle, where you retain some sweetness and new flavor compounds, but without the bitterness.

So, no, you don't need a recipe to tell you how to make a s'more, but rather just a reminder to be patient, keep your marshmallow out of the flames, and let science do the work until you've achieved golden-brown, caramelized s'more perfection.

GIANT OATMEAL TRAIL MIX COOKIES

Use a store-bought trail mix or make your own, whichever you prefer. One of the keys to this recipe is the brown butter—it's perfectly okay to simply use melted butter or vegetable oil, but the extra step of browning the butter only takes a few minutes and brings out a toasty, caramelly, nutty flavor. Believe me, once you use brown butter in cookies, you'll never go back.

YIELDS	CAMPING STYLE	DIETARY NOTES
Makes 10 large (5-inch) cookies	Backcountry 🥾	Vegetarian 𝛷

1 cup butter (2 sticks)
2 eggs
1½ cups brown sugar
1 teaspoon salt
2 teaspoons vanilla extract
2½ cups quick oats

1½ cups all-purpose flour
½ cup trail mix of your choice
1 cup dark chocolate chips
2 teaspoons baking soda
Pinch flaky sea salt

Home prep: Preheat oven to 350°F. Put butter in a saucepan over medium heat and cook, stirring frequently. It will start to foam and darken after a few minutes. Continue to stir and cook until foam has subsided and butter has turned golden brown, being careful not to scorch it, 5–8 minutes total. You should notice a distinct change in the color and a rich, nutty aroma. Remove from heat, set aside, and cool for about 10 minutes before using.

Stir brown butter in with eggs, brown sugar, salt, and vanilla extract and mix until well beaten. Add remaining ingredients (except sea salt) and mix until well combined. Scoop ½ cup dough for each cookie onto a parchment-lined baking sheet, about 3 inches apart from each other. Press to flatten slightly (think hockey puck–shaped), then sprinkle each cookie with a pinch of flaky sea salt. Bake 12–15 minutes, or until cookies spread out and flatten but are still soft (if you prefer a crunchier cookie, bake 3–5 minutes longer). Cool on a wire rack and store in an airtight container.

At camp: Take on the trail for a protein-packed treat, or use as a substitute for graham crackers in s'mores (p. 167).

Desserts

MULLED CIDER

Whether you want to fortify some instant hot cider or have a cooler to bring your own fresh batch, this warming spice-blend creates the perfect sip for a cool summer night or fall morning. You don't have to wrap the spices in cheesecloth, but doing so makes packing, serving, and cleaning up a breeze.

YIELDS	CAMPING STYLE	EQUIPMENT	DIETARY NOTES
Serves 4	Backcountry 🚶	Lightweight cook set Backpacking stove Cheesecloth	Vegan Gluten-free Dairy-free

2 cinnamon sticks, 3-inch
6 whole cloves
1 whole star anise
10 whole allspice berries
1 orange, sliced
4 cups apple cider
6 ounces rum, optional
Cinnamon sticks, for serving

Home prep: Wrap spices in a piece of cheesecloth and tie a knot or use butchers' twine to keep wrapped. Pack other ingredients separately.

At camp: Combine spices, sliced orange, and cider in a pot and bring to a simmer over medium heat, 5–10 minutes, then remove from heat. Divide rum, if desired, between 4 mugs, then add cider and a cinnamon stick to each mug to serve.

DARK CHOCOLATE–BLUEBERRY BANANA BOATS (FOIL PACKET)

Banana boats are a true "choose-your-own-adventure" dessert, making them a real crowd-pleaser. Start with this recipe for inspiration, or simply use this method combined with your own choice of toppings. These are best prepared in camp, otherwise the cut banana will turn brown.

YIELDS	CAMPING STYLE	EQUIPMENT	DIETARY NOTES
Serves 6	Frontcountry 🚗	Metal grill tongs Aluminum foil Hot campfire coals	Vegetarian ⌀

6 fresh bananas
6 ounces fresh blueberries
Dark chocolate chips
Mini marshmallows

Home prep: Pack all ingredients separately.

At camp: Prepare a campfire for cooking in foil packets (see p. 109). Meanwhile, slice each banana lengthwise and open like a book, leaving the peel on. Divide blueberries evenly between bananas, then top with a handful of chocolate chips and mini marshmallows. Individually wrap each banana tightly in foil, then cook over hot coals, rotating with tongs occasionally, until marshmallows and chocolate are melted and blueberries are syrupy, about 15 minutes.

Desserts

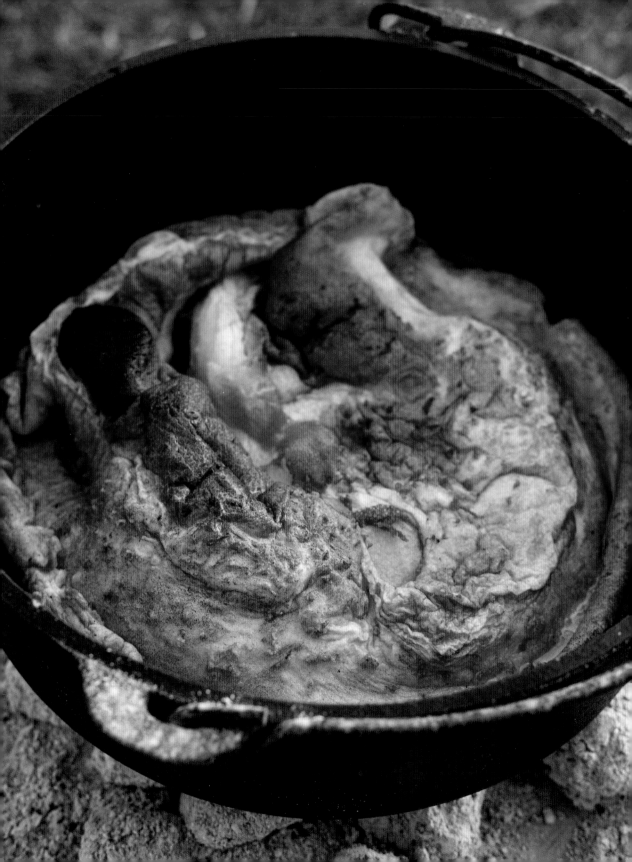

DUTCH BABY

A Dutch baby, sometimes referred to as a German pancake, is a puffy, custardy pancake that works just as well for a slow brunch as it does for a crowd-pleasing dessert. One of the tricks to getting it to puff up is to let the dough come to room temperature before cooking. Serve with Nutella, berries, or simply with some powdered sugar and maple syrup.

YIELDS	CAMPING STYLE	EQUIPMENT	DIETARY NOTES
Serves 6	Frontcountry 🚗	Dutch oven Charcoal chimney starter (or hot campfire coals)	Vegetarian ⌀

3 eggs
½ cup milk
2 tablespoons sugar
1 teaspoon vanilla extract
½ cup flour
4 tablespoons butter
Optional toppings: powdered sugar, jam, berries, Nutella, maple syrup

Home prep: Beat eggs and mix with milk, sugar, and vanilla extract. Stir in flour and mix until well combined. Pack butter separately. Batter can be made up to a day ahead of time and stored in a cooler or refrigerator (let come to room temperature before baking).

At camp: Prepare ¾ of a chimney full of charcoal. When coals are lit, place half underneath the Dutch oven on a fireproof surface and the other half on top of the lid. Let the oven preheat until hot, 5–7 minutes.

When the oven is hot, add the butter. As soon as it has melted, add batter and replace the lid. Bake until pancake is puffy and golden brown but still custardy on the inside, about 20 minutes, checking halfway through to ensure it hasn't puffed up so much that it's pressed against the lid (lifting the lid will make it deflate slightly). Let cool slightly, then cut into wedges and serve with your choice of toppings.

PEACH AND OAT CRISP

Nearly any fruit will work with this sweet, crunchy treat—just use about 2 cups of whatever you've foraged or can find in season. If you're car camping and have a cooler, thawed frozen fruit works well too. For a richer dessert, swap out the coconut oil for butter.

YIELDS	CAMPING STYLE	EQUIPMENT	DIETARY NOTES
Serves 2	Frontcountry 🚗	Cast-iron or nonstick skillet Backpacking stove or two-burner stove	Vegan Dairy-free

2 tablespoons coconut oil, divided
½ cup rolled oats
1 tablespoon brown sugar
2 fresh peaches, sliced (or 2 cups fruit total)
1 tablespoon brown sugar
1 tablespoon all-purpose flour
1½ ounces rum or bourbon, optional

Home prep: Pack all ingredients separately.

At camp: Heat 1 tablespoon of the coconut oil in a skillet over medium heat, then add oats and brown sugar. Cook, stirring frequently, until oats are lightly toasted and browned. Remove from heat and set aside in a separate bowl.

Return skillet to stove and heat remaining 1 tablespoon coconut oil over medium heat. Add fruit, brown sugar, and flour, and cook, stirring frequently, until mixture has thickened slightly and flour is incorporated, about 5 minutes. Add alcohol if desired, then continue to cook until fruit is lightly browned and caramelized, another 5 minutes. Divide between two bowls and top with toasted oats.

ORANGE CHOCOLATE BROWNIES (FOIL PACKET)

Hollowed-out oranges are the perfect vessels for brownies, infusing them with a floral, citrusy flavor that works surprisingly well. While hollowing out the oranges takes a bit of work, using boxed brownie batter helps keep the prep work to a minimum. One box of batter is enough to fill about 6 oranges.

YIELDS	CAMPING STYLE	EQUIPMENT	DIETARY NOTES
Serves 6	Frontcountry	Metal grill tongs	Vegetarian
	🚗	Aluminum foil	∅
		Hot campfire coals	

6 oranges
1 box brownie batter of your choice (and additional
   ingredients according to package instructions)

Home prep: Cut off the top quarter of the oranges, saving tops. Using a knife, cut as close as you can along the inside of orange to cut out the flesh, then use a spoon to scrape out the rest (save orange flesh for another use). When oranges are hollowed out, mix brownie batter according to box directions, then divide batter evenly among oranges. You'll want to fill each about ¾ of the way full, leaving room for batter to expand. Replace tops on each orange, then individually wrap each orange tightly in foil, crimping seams of foil. Wrap in another sheet of foil, then store in a cooler or refrigerator until ready to cook. The oranges and batter can be prepared a day or two ahead of time.

At camp: Prepare a campfire for cooking in foil packets (see p. 109). Cook over hot coals, rotating with tongs occasionally, until brownie batter is cooked, about 30 minutes.

ACKNOWLEDGMENTS

This book wouldn't have been possible without help from my family, friends, and editors. I owe it to my parents, Paul and Dori, for sharing their love of cooking (and eating) with me. Amanda and Ned Pinkerton were the first to introduce me to Dutch oven cooking, turning out stews and breads on Boy Scout camping trips and beyond (they also kindly lent me their very large, very loud dehydrator for writing this book).

It was former *Backpacker* editor Corey Buhay who first convinced me to start developing recipes for backpacking and who gave me an outlet to get started. Without that, I wouldn't have built up the experience or confidence to take on a whole book project.

It was with former CMC editor Jeff Golden's encouragement that I pitched this book, and I thank him for seeing in me the potential to pull this off. He passed the baton on to CMC's director of publishing, Sarah Gorecki, and editor, Casey Blaine, who patiently guided me through to the end and made sense of my ramblings.

And finally, thanks to my partner, Emy Scherrer, and all my friends who taste tested and tagged along with me for field testing.

ABOUT THE AUTHOR

Nick Cote is a journalist and photographer based in Bellingham, Washington. He has taught photojournalism at the University of Colorado, Boulder, and has done recipe research on the trail for *Backpacker* and REI Co-op Journal. His work has also been published in the *New York Times,* the *Washington Post,* the *Wall Street Journal, Outside,* and many other publications. When not in the kitchen, you can find him taking advantage of the Pacific Northwest's amazing trails, rivers, mountains, and beaches.

Photo by Emy Scherrer

Illustration by Jesse Crock

Join Today.
Adventure Tomorrow.

The Colorado Mountain Club is the Rocky Mountain community for mountain education, adventure, and conservation. We bring people together to share our love of the mountains. We value our community and go out of our way to welcome and include all Coloradoans—from the uninitiated to the expert, there is a place for everyone here.

cmc.org